The Four G
and other t

A Critical Handbook of the New Testament

Dick Butler

Published by the Barbican Press,
21 Defoe House,
Barbican,
London EC2Y 8DN
Telephone: 020 7628 0527
Email: barbicanpress@btinternet.com
Website: www.the-four-gospels.co.uk

ISBN No: 978-0-9554861-0-4

First published June 2007

Extracts from the New English Bible, copyright Oxford and
Cambridge University Presses 1961, 1970, reproduced by kind
permission

Cover design by Leigh Hurlock

The cover design incorporates an image of the Codex Sinaiticus
(discussed on page 146) and reproduced by kind permission of the
British Library. It shows the opening page of the Gospel according
to John.

Printed by Page Bros (Norwich) Ltd,
Mile Cross Lane
Norwich NR6 6SA

TABLE OF CONTENTS

The New Testament in use

Two Old Testament Texts

Appendices

Indexes

INTRODUCTION

FINDING OUT FOR ONESELF

This book has its origins in a series of Fact Sheets, which I wrote for my last Anglican parish. They were freely available on the Church Bookstall for anyone to take and, as their title suggests, the aim was to provide basic information on topics of church interest. Visiting clergy of a conservative disposition were often shocked by them (I was a heretic in their eyes), but visitors who arrived early for weddings and funerals would commonly stand around the Bookstall reading them, and often left with a handful. Basic information about Christian belief can be very difficult to come by.

Sermons are ephemeral and rarely get to grips with core beliefs or texts. So it is possible to attend churches for a lifetime and never hear many of the texts and subjects discussed in this Handbook analysed or, even, referred to. Christmas and Easter can pass year after year without any attempt being made to look objectively at the Birth Narratives or the story of the Empty Tomb. The words "Synoptic Gospels" may not mean anything, yet are so crucial for an understanding of the life of Jesus. Discussion Groups can be just as disappointing. They are frequently confrontational and the shy and less well informed feel at a disadvantage in them. They tend to deal in opinions rather than facts. So my hope in writing the original Fact Sheets, in response to a Church Council discussion, was that those who took them could read them at home without getting upset, and could reflect upon their contents without feeling under pressure. Their aim was not to persuade, but to inform.

But it is silly to pretend that Christian belief is uncontroversial. Even in the New Testament there is evidence of conflict and, in churches today, subjects that are in the least controversial are almost always avoided. The last thing that any church leader wants to do is to open a debate about Christian belief in which his, or her, own beliefs are challenged

1

as unorthodox. At the least it causes hurt to those who disagree, and at worst it brings huge media pressure, with many unwanted telephone calls and invitations to appear on television. Even today Anglican clergy can lose their jobs for stepping out of line, and the quiet life has many attractions. Heresy remains a charge that we all fear. And objectivity is difficult. It is indeed true that we all approach facts (and indeed you, dear Reader, this book) from a particular point of view. So, to address this objection, I have included a brief theological autobiography, so that those of you who want to do so can place me within the spectrum of church opinion. It will give you an angle on what I write.

In other disciplines the principal problem in establishing facts is lack of evidence and, inevitably, since Christian faith pre-dates the modern era, there will be many things that we cannot know for certain. This will be particularly true of the life of Jesus. But we need not give up on facts altogether. Some facts can be established beyond reasonable doubt, and these must be honoured.

A priori beliefs and old loyalties

Why, then, are facts often so contentious, when reasonable people might be expected to agree? Scientists or historians do not disagree about fundamentals in the way that Christian historians and apologists do. Sadly, the reason for this is that few Christians approach the facts at issue with an open mind. They have a priori beliefs, often instilled in childhood, which predispose them to a certain view, even when the evidence points in a different direction. So, for example, it is a question of fact whether Jesus had brothers and sisters, or not. All the evidence is that he did. He had four brothers and an indeterminate number of sisters. We even know the names of the brothers and that some of them, at least, were married (see the chapter on *Jesus' Family and Friends*). Why then should these facts be disputed? It is because, whatever the evidence, those who have been brought up within certain traditions cannot believe that it is possible. They have a priori beliefs with which the new facts cannot be reconciled. So to accept that Jesus had brothers and sisters would conflict with everything that

2

Catholic and Orthodox Christians have ever been taught. Do crib scenes ever include little brothers and sisters, uncles and aunts, nephews and nieces, amongst Jesus' family circle? It is right that *a priori* beliefs should be respected, and it is sensible, in the first instance, to be more sceptical of facts which do not fit in with what we already believe. But sometimes new facts cannot be denied and have to be assimilated into our picture of the world, whatever the disturbance and the fallout may be. To cling obstinately to *a priori* beliefs in the face of clear evidence that they are mistaken is to give up on theology altogether.

Another commonly held *a priori* belief, shared by conservative Christians of all traditions, is that the Bible is the infallible Word of God and true in every particular. Such Christians are often referred to (although not by themselves) as Fundamentalists, and Fundamentalism precludes textual criticism. Yet the Bible is a text that can be studied like any other text, and conclusions drawn. So all the evidence (the evidence of the texts themselves, that is) suggests that the first three Gospels have common sources and are not the individual accounts of eyewitnesses. And if this is true, Matthew's Gospel cannot have been written by Matthew the disciple, to whom it is attributed. Indeed, worse than that in the eyes of some, it now appears, as I hope to show, that the Synoptic Gospels are effectively re-writes of one another.

Fighting for a cause

A further complication is that church life is highly partisan. Each of the official churches is in the market to retain and win new members, and a case has therefore to be presented and argued on their behalf. The nearest analogy is with politics. In politics no one ever admits to being wrong, and objectivity is a total bar to participation. As a result no one ever accepts what any party spokesman says uncritically, except those who already support the cause. Politicians, who rely upon public support, have to present a case, to persuade, to "put a spin" upon the facts.

And Christians do the same. Loyalty plays a huge part in religious allegiance. Many people, in fact, are incapable of changing or adapting at all. The religious map of the world, which includes people of all religions and none, will show boundaries and frontiers like the political map. And, by and large, most people are true to their inheritance. A few may cross frontiers to join another allegiance, but the major re-shaping of religious, as well as of political, boundaries has, in the past, almost always been a consequence of war, or emigration. Facts and debate have occasionally played a part, but are very rarely decisive. But today making up your own mind is more possible than ever before, and this Handbook seeks to be helpful to those of an independent spirit who want to find out things for themselves. It will, no doubt, be disputed by many, and by some in very emotional terms. Inevitably it will contain some errors and these will need correction. But not all criticism will be objective and rational. I have to be prepared for this, but I am fortunate to live in a tolerant and liberal society where the sanctions that can be applied to a retired clergyman are very few indeed.

So the primary purpose of this Handbook, as of the Fact Sheets before them, is to provide accurate and dispassionate information, so that those who want to know more have somewhere to turn.

THE *CRITICAL* STUDY OF TEXTS

I thought to include this short section to explain the use of the word "critical" in the subtitle of the book. It can have a negative connotation. If a person is critical of something, it usually means that they find fault with it, or think it mistaken. So criticism denotes a hostile attitude and is hurtful in personal terms. We want to be liked and not criticised, and that applies to every aspect of our lives – our appearance, our personal qualities, our families, but most of all our opinions and beliefs. Few words please us more than, "I think that you are absolutely right!" *Private Eye* had a cartoon some years ago of a beggar sitting on the pavement with the placard: "Your opinions confirmed. 10p per opinion." Even the paid support of a beggar can be reassuring.

Criticism, however, need not be negative. Theatre critics may criticise the plays they review, but will also point to their strengths. Actors and actresses, naturally, will hate critics because they only want to hear good things. Professionally, the success of their career, as well as of the actual production, may rest upon it. Criticism can be particularly hurtful and devastating when it is ill-informed or vindictive. Who are critics to criticise, anyway, when they cannot act themselves? But even the critics' role is difficult. They have an editor and readers to please as well.

Theology may seem a world away from the theatre, but the role of the theologian can be quite as hazardous as that of the actor or playwright. In the not-too-distant past the penalty for heresy was execution! Yet criticism is as necessary in theology as anywhere else, and can be as objective. It can help us evaluate, bringing out the strengths of beliefs and texts, as well as their weaknesses. Traditionally, however, religious texts and doctrines have been thought of as *above* criticism. *Sacred* Scriptures (the Koran in the eyes of Muslims, the Bible in Christian eyes) are thought to be of divine origin, inspired by God, perhaps even written by God. So to criticise the Bible or the Koran is blasphemous. No one can argue with God, and if the Bible is the divinely inspired Word of God, then all criticism of it is out of place. Every word must be equally true and without error. Even translation is misconceived and wrong. And to emphasise the authority of Scripture, the physical text (the actual book) is often gilded, bound in fine leather, sometimes embellished with precious stones, and is carried in solemn procession. Can such a book have mistakes in it, or be criticised? "Of course, not!" the fundamentalist replies. I remember, once, inviting a Jewish scholar to a study group in which we were discussing what *we* called "the Old Testament". At one point, and to make room for something else, I placed an Old Testament on the carpet. He quickly picked it up – the floor is no place for the divinely inspired Scriptures.

This Handbook will be anathema to such as he, and there are fundamentalist Christians as well as orthodox Jews. But in a democracy nothing is above criticism. The divine authority of the Bible goes the same way as the divine right of kings. In a democracy we are all entitled to our own view and we will judge as we find. And so we begin to study a text more closely. We need open minds, but the eyes of a hawk as well. So we begin to question. Does our reading of the Gospel according to Matthew support the traditional view that it was written by Matthew the disciple? In my view it does not, but in itself this does not belittle the Gospel in any way. Its author (and we still call him Matthew for convenience) was a scholar ("a Scribe", he would have said) of extraordinary brilliance, so that, paradoxically, we can respect Matthew's Gospel even more when we have studied it closely, than when we have merely accepted it as divinely inspired.

There are also analogies with art criticism. An art critic looks, of course, at the front of a picture, but is interested in the back as well. In fact he looks at it from every angle. He compares it with other pictures. He tries to place it in context. And this is his expertise – he knows from experience whether a picture was painted in the sixteenth or eighteenth century, and what its provenance is. Someone who has not studied art or painting cannot do this, or cannot do it as accurately. And this is also true of Biblical Criticism. We study, and compare, and contextualise. We lift the corners, and look in the margins, and compare manuscripts, but most of all (the key to all Gospel criticism) we compare one Gospel with another. And the result of our doing this has been both surprising and controversial.

While Rector of my old church in south east London, I several times went, by invitation, to Bible Breakfasts at my local Pentecostal Church, where the speaker would hold up his Bible and proclaim it to be "the infallible Word of God". I was known to have other views, and might perhaps be converted. But my fault, in their pastor's view, was to have read the Bible *too* closely, and to make its exposition *too* complicated. For in the eyes of many the outcome of studying religious texts and doctrines critically has been to diminish them. It becomes a process whereby we are left with less at the end than we began with. The more fearful may even feel that we shall be left with nothing, for once the process has begun it cannot be halted. You cannot un-think thoughts once you have thought them. This is why the Roman Catholic Church, in particular, defends every position, because to yield to criticism at any single point is to weaken the structure as a whole. My view is that we can learn to live with less (the whole thrust of modernism and minimalism in every subject), while still admiring the achievements of earlier generations, whose views were inevitably different from ours. For theological doctrines and texts can be dated and contextualised like any piece of furniture. Puritanism was a sixteenth and seventeenth-century response to the Reformation, Deism an eighteenth-century response to the rise of science. I admire them both. I might have been a Puritan or a Deist, had I lived then. But I do not have that choice. I am a twenty-first-century man and I can only be myself. And, if our studies reduce, so be it. But they will also enhance. Some texts will survive our critical scrutiny, and our admiration for them will then be greater than before. What we are left with may sometimes be less, but it will also be more precious.

THE GOSPELS

THE SYNOPTIC GOSPELS

The Synoptic Gospels are Mark, Matthew and Luke. So, by implication, John's Gospel is excluded. It is *not* a Synoptic Gospel. The word "Synoptic" derives from the Greek word *sun* meaning "together", and *opsis* meaning "a view". The Synoptic Gospels can be "viewed together". They not only have many of the same stories, but mostly have them in the same order with, in many cases, a word-for-word correspondence. They can therefore be set out in columns, as in Huck's famous Greek *Synopsis of the First Three Gospels*[1]. The exact extent of the correspondence can then be seen. A Table of Synoptic Parallels is appended to this chapter.

Traditional Views

Before Biblical Criticism the Evangelists were taken to be eye-witnesses, or near eye-witnesses, of the events they describe. Matthew's and John's Gospels were assumed to have been written by the disciples, Matthew and John. Mark, according to Eusebius of Caesarea[2], was believed to have derived his material from Peter (*The History of the Church Book 2, Section 14*), while Luke's Gospel was thought to be the Gospel which Paul regarded as his own (*Book 3, Section 4*).

But, ultimately, all four Gospels were bound together and came to be regarded as sacred texts. No distinction was then drawn between them. They were all Gospels, of equal authority, and complementary to one another. *The Tome of Leo*[3], which dates from AD 449, assembled a selection of texts to show that Jesus was both human and divine. The sayings of Jesus adduced as proof of his humanity were taken from the Synoptic Gospels, while the sayings pointing to his divinity were taken from John's Gospel. But, at the time, no one realised the significance of this. In fact, the comparative study of the Gospels would have been all but impossible before the invention of printing.

Biblical Criticism and the Priority of Mark

Biblical Criticism is the scholarly study of the Bible to determine the authorship, sources, and relationship of its different books and, broadly, may be said to date from the publication of David Friedrich Strauss' *Life of Jesus* in 1835[4]. It proved both a very popular and a very controversial book. Strauss set out to discover the real Jesus, whom he believed to have been obscured by centuries of dogma and devotion, and it launched what has come to be known as the *Quest for the Historical Jesus*[5]. Its first discovery was, indeed, that the Synoptic Gospels stand apart from John's Gospel in sharing common sources, since a close comparison of near identical stories proves there to have been copying. And why should an eyewitness need to copy from someone else, if he has his own personal recollection of what happened? The Gospels cannot, therefore, have been written by disciples, whatever their attribution. So the hunt was on for sources.

This approach was attractive because it would imply that, while not written by disciples, the Gospels still had a sure historical basis. So the first task was to decide in what order the three Gospels were written and ultimately to establish the priority of Mark. Mark stands second to Matthew in the New Testament and, until very recently, was little regarded. It is much the shortest of the Synoptic Gospels and lacks so much that the other two Synoptic Gospels include. It has no Birth Narratives, no Resurrection Appearances, no Sermon on the Mount, and very few parables. It was no one's favourite Gospel and was very little read. Yet the internal evidence for its having been written first is conclusive. Matthew and Luke include almost all of Mark's material, while his lacks so much of theirs.

The Four Document Hypothesis

While all of this was an exciting discovery for some, it was bad news for others. Many people would have preferred the evangelists to have been disciples but, if they were not, it was important that they each had reliable historical sources, and preferably *written* rather than oral ones. There was no evidence for these, but it was assumed that they must have existed.

So Mark was said to have had *UrMarkus* as his source (*UrMarkus* is German for "Primitive Mark"). Matthew, it was thought, must have had three sources - Mark, M (M for Matthew, his own unique source), and Q (from *Quelle*, the German for "Source" - the material he and Luke shared, but which is not found in Mark). Luke was also thought to have had three sources - Mark (again), L (L for Luke, or *Proto-Luke*, his unique source) and Q again (the source he shared with Matthew). So, to summarise, *four* written sources (*UrMarkus*, M, L and Q) were thought to underlie the Synoptic Gospels. There was nothing to prove that any of them actually existed, but psychologically they were important in indicating that the stories about Jesus in the Synoptic Gospels had historical roots. The thinking behind Q was a conviction that Matthew and Luke worked completely separately and that neither knew the other's Gospel. If, therefore, they have common material not found in Mark (the story of the temptation of Jesus, for example), they must have found it elsewhere - in Q. All of this was called the Four Document Hypothesis. It set out to explain the common material in the three Synoptic Gospels.

The Four Document Hypothesis held the field for more than 100 years and is associated in the United Kingdom with B.H.Streeter's *The Four Gospels*, published in 1924. But it was speculative (Q, in particular, lacked substance or rationale) and it diminished the stature of the evangelists themselves. They were reduced to the role of editor, and rather ineffective editors at that, since there was thought to be no logic to the order in which they had retold the stories. For another feature of the Synoptic Gospels, which sets them apart from John, is that the individual units, or *pericope*[6] (from the Greek for "section"), are quite short. All that the evangelists had done, on the Four Document Hypothesis, was to thread these short stories "like beads on a string", and in a somewhat random fashion. It was suggested that they did not really know what they were doing. Twentieth-century Biblical scholars knew better!

A New Paradigm[7]

The first serious challenge to the traditional theory came with the publication of an article by Austin Farrer[8], called

"Dispensing with Q". And Michael Goulder[9] (in *Midrash and Lection in Matthew*, and in *Luke, a new Paradigm*) has now proposed an original and convincing alternative theory. The challenge all along has been to suggest a simpler explanation of the relationship between the Synoptic Gospels, which did not require recourse to hypothetical sources. And the new paradigm is this: that Mark wrote first; that Matthew rewrote Mark, adding new material of his own; and that Luke wrote third, conflating Matthew and Mark, and adding new material of *his* own again. And, to put it precisely, *almost* all (perhaps *all*) of this new material is midrash. Mark, Matthew and Luke were not editors after all, but authors or, as they would have thought of themselves, Scribes[10]. They sought to explain, expand, and embellish, finding inspiration in Old Testament texts and stories, as well as in each other's Gospels.

Unsurprisingly this view has not proved welcome or popular with conservative scholars, although few have yet ventured to refute it. It is a much simpler explanation of the relationship between the Synoptic Gospels, but the problem is that it seems to undermine the historicity of many of the Gospel stories. Conservative Christians will probably always remain loyal to the view that the Gospels were written by eye-witnesses, and indeed by the people to whom they are attributed, whatever the evidence to the contrary. But even some liberal scholars have been alarmed to discover how great a part midrash has played in the re-telling of the story of Jesus. Yet the new paradigm has proved immensely illuminating and has led to the resolution of other problems as well. No one can say that further progress in Biblical studies will not be made, but the Four Document Hypothesis is now seriously disputed. The assumption of non-existent documents is unnecessary.

Glossing

The key to everything lies in a minute comparison of individual texts. This has come to be known as Redaction Criticism, although the term has never been widely used. From the baptism of Jesus onwards (the first story in Mark's Gospel), Huck identified perhaps 50 stories (*pericope*) which occur in *each* of the Synoptic Gospels, and in the *same* order. It is difficult to be more specific, because it is not always possible to be absolutely certain where one story ends and another begins. And then, in addition, there are the stories which occur in *two* Gospels, but not in all three, and those which are *common to all three* but occur in a *different order*. What is indisputable is that the three Gospels have a huge amount of shared material, and that almost all of Mark's Gospel is common to at least one of the other two.

If all these stories are set side by side, the evidence for copying is incontrovertible. Not just the things that Jesus said, which could be expected to be the same if accurately reported, but much of the editorial material as well is either identical or very similar. Yet there are differences, too. We rarely copy anything exactly. Every author has his own favourite words and style. He may have a problem with some of his material, or think some of it too long. He may feel that other stories require amplification or explanation. He may also have his own overview of the story which he is retelling. So he glosses and, if all these glosses are taken together over a whole Gospel, a consistent pattern emerges. Mark had his theological overview and distinctive style, Matthew his, and Luke his. They each have favourite words and, when account is taken of this glossing, they begin to emerge as authors in their own right. Matthew and Luke want to be faithful to Mark, but there is a degree of consistent reinterpretation as well. So, in comparing three similar accounts of the same incident, and bearing in mind the order in which we believe the Gospels to have been written, we are looking for fingerprints. We all leave them wherever we go, in what we write as much as in what we touch.

An Illustration of Glossing

As illustration, we could compare just a single verse in each of the Gospels: Mark 15.21; Matthew 27.32; Luke 23.26. It is part of the Passion Narrative. Mark's version translates (literally):

"And they pressed into service a certain Simon a Cyrenian passing by coming from the country the father of Alexander and Rufus in order that he might take up the cross of him."

This gives nineteen Greek words (there is no punctuation in the oldest complete manuscripts, no break between words, and the text throughout is in upper case).

Now the evidence for copying is cumulative, but in this verse Matthew has fourteen words altogether, of which the last five are *identical* to Mark's ("in order that he might take up the cross of him"); five are left out ("the father of Alexander and Rufus"); three words provide a link with what went before and help the sense ("Coming out they discovered"); and one word (a verb) is the same but in a different tense.

Luke has:

"And as they led him away, seizing a certain Simon, a Cyrenian, coming from the country, they put on him the cross to bear behind Jesus".

This gives nineteen Greek words. Disregarding Simon's name and "the cross", three words are identical ("coming from the country"), five are left out ("the father of Alexander and Rufus"), while most of the others are similar.

The analysis of a single verse will not convince the sceptical, but can help to illustrate how texts can be glossed. So, in this verse, can we guess what has prompted the glosses that Matthew and Luke have made, since they do not copy Mark *exactly*, from beginning to end, word for word? The addition of link words, to bed a section into their Gospels, is common. It is part of the process of joining up sections seamlessly. Matthew's "coming out they discovered" falls into this category.

Then, both Matthew and Luke leave out "the father of Alexander and Rufus". Here a simple explanation might be that, while Mark adds "the father of Alexander and Rufus" to help identify Simon to *his* readers, Matthew's and Luke's readers might not have known who Alexander or Rufus were. So it would be confusing to complicate things unnecessarily by including their names.

But, most interestingly of all, Luke adds that Simon walked "behind" Jesus. Superficially we might take this to be a simple descriptive addition. Luke was helping his readers to picture the scene. Did Simon walk in front of Jesus, beside him, or behind him? The answer is "behind him". But much more probably (these things can never be proved) Luke had a

13

theological purpose. For him Jesus is the great exemplar of discipleship and those who would be Jesus' disciples must take up their cross every day (Luke 9.23) and *follow* him (*not* walk in front of him, or beside him). Both Matthew and Luke often have a theological motif such as this in glossing a text.

The Old Testament as a Further Source

So Matthew and Luke rewrote Mark, copying, but at the same time glossing. Sometimes the glossing will have been conscious, sometimes unconscious. Theirs are, however, much longer Gospels than Mark's and the question remains as to where all the extra material has come from. According to the Four Document Hypothesis, they drew upon three further written sources – M, L, and Q (the shared source). A much simpler explanation is that their only further written source is one to which we, too, have access – the Old Testament. Both Matthew and Luke believed that Jesus had fulfilled both the Law and the Prophets (and not just the Prophets). They are quite specific. Matthew has Jesus say, at the beginning of the Sermon on the Mount: "Do not suppose that I have come to abolish the Law and the Prophets; I did not come to abolish, but to fulfil" (Matthew 5.17). Luke even adds the Psalms, since they represent a further division of the Old Testament. In the reprise at the end of his Gospel he has the Risen Jesus say to his disciples: "This is what I meant by saying, while I was still with you, that *everything* written about me in the *Law of Moses* and in the *prophets* and *psalms* was bound to be fulfilled" (Luke 24.44). Where should a Christian Scribe look to fill out the story of Jesus, but to the Scriptures?

However, their idea of fulfilment is commonly misunderstood today. It was not simply that the prophets had predicted that something would happen (say, that Jesus would be born in Bethlehem) and then (lo, and behold) it *does* happen (Jesus *is* born in Bethlehem). Rather, the *whole* of the Old Testament is a sourcebook for the story of Jesus, the narratives and psalms as well as the books of prophecy. So Jesus fulfils the Old Testament by embodying its heroes. Jesus is another Moses - he delivers the Sermon on the Mount, reinterpreting the Mosaic Law and radicalizing it (Matthew 5 - 7). He is another

Samuel, disputing with the teachers in the temple while still a child (1 Samuel 3 and Luke 2. 41-52). He is another Solomon, preaching in parables, yet wiser even than Solomon was (1 Kings 10. 1-10 and Matthew 12.42). He is another Jonah, rising from the dead after three days, as Jonah rose from the raging sea, after three days in the belly of the sea monster (Matthew 12. 38-41). He is another Elisha, feeding the crowds with bread as Elisha had done (2 Kings 4. 42-44). In each case Jesus is the fulfilment of an Old Testament hero. Moses, Samuel, Solomon, Jonah and Elisha are "types" of Jesus and so, to embellish and expand their gospels, Mark, Matthew and Luke had recourse to the Old Testament stories in which these "types" feature. In each case Jesus is their fulfilment. And, in the same way John the Baptist is another Elijah, Mary another Hannah. Matthew and Luke had no need to feel short of material. Heroes and heroines of every kind lay to hand in the Old Testament.

Midrash

"Midrash" is a Biblical word and occurs twice in the Old Testament at 2 Chronicles 13.22 and 24.27. It derives from the Hebrew word *darash*, meaning to probe or examine. The preacher or rabbi looks beneath the surface of Scripture to discover new truths and new stories within it. He uncovers hidden layers of meaning which were not previously apparent. He amplifies, and explains, and reconciles. We would regard it as a creative process, but the Scribe would not think of himself as being at liberty to write whatever he wished. He must be true to the texts he is expounding, although sometimes the need would arise to align old texts with present practice and belief, where contradictions arose.

Much of the Old Testament is also itself the outcome of midrash. So Deuteronomy (literally the Second Law) is a midrash of Exodus. Exodus is the older book and contains the earlier forms of the Law. Deuteronomy expounds that Law in a series of discourses, which its author attributes to Moses, but which reflect the insights of the eighth and seventh centuries BC. Leviticus (literally, the book of the Levites) is a further, later midrash which reflects the views of the Priestly School, which was the dominant party in fifth and fourth centuries BC, after

15

the Exile. So these three books (Exodus, Deuteronomy, and Leviticus) represent an evolving tradition whereby the Law is corrected and amplified. The same is true of the books which tell the story of Israel's history. The Deuteronomic history in 1 and 2 Samuel, and 1 and 2 Kings (1 - 4 Kingdoms in the Hebrew Bible) tells the story of the monarchy from Saul to the destruction of Jerusalem in 586 BC, and from the same point of view as the author of Deuteronomy. But this history was midrashed, corrected, and brought up to date by the Chronicler (the author of 1 and 2 Chronicles), who, like Ezra and Nehemiah, belonged to the Priestly School. So, effectively, Deuteronomy and Leviticus are successive re-writes of Exodus, while 1 and 2 Chronicles are a re-write of the books of Samuel and Kings.

In the same way there are successive re-writes of the Christian Gospel. Mark will have had historical sources, although their precise extent is difficult to determine. But he, too, midrashed and his account of the story of the beheading of John the Baptist (Mark 6. 14-29) is an uncontroversial example, since he actually quotes from the story in Esther, which he is midrashing. Herod's promise to his daughter ("Whatever you ask I will give you, up to half my kingdom") is the exact promise which King Ahasuerus made to Esther (Esther 5.3). Midrash is rarely simple, but it is beyond doubt that the story of Esther was in Mark's mind when he told the story of the death of John the Baptist. He was midrashing.

The problem in Mark's case is that we do not have access to his historical sources, whether written or oral. But in Matthew and Luke's cases we do. So we can see exactly what they are doing. Mark is Matthew's historical source, while Mark and Matthew are Luke's. Where each adds material of his own, therefore, it will be midrash. Many examples will be found in the following chapters, but the Birth Narratives provide a first example and a separate chapter is devoted to them. So, for the present, we note that although Mark's, Matthew's and Luke's Gospels differ in many respects, they also have a great deal in common, as the appended table shows. And that is why they are referred to as the Synoptic Gospels.

[1] Albert Huck was a German New Testament scholar and his Greek *Synopsis of the first three Gospels* was published in 1892 and has been many times revised. There are also English Synopses available today, which are helpful to those without Greek, but do not allow the comparison of individual words as a Greek Synopsis does. Another hugely helpful aid to Biblical Studies is Robert Young's *Analytical Concordance to the Holy Bible*, first published in 1879, which lists every occurrence of every word in both the Greek, and English Authorized Version, of the Bible. These two books, together with Westcott and Hort's critical edition of the Greek New Testament, which was published in 1881, laid the foundation for scholarly Biblical Criticism.

[2] Eusebius of Caesarea (AD *c*.260-340) was one of the leading churchmen of his day and a prolific author. He escaped the Diocletian Persecution and, much as John Foxe was to do in his *Acts and Monuments* and Alexander Solzhenitsyn in his *Gulag Archipelago*, wrote the *History of the Church from Christ to Constantine* to honour those who had been martyred in the cause. It is an invaluable source of early texts, which he quotes in full, and is available as a Penguin paperback. Eusebius also attended the Council of Nicaea in AD 325, and in AD 336 gave the address at the celebrations to mark the thirtieth anniversary of Constantine's becoming Emperor. He was clearly Constantine's favourite bishop.

[3] *The Tome of Leo* is a letter of some six pages written by Leo I to Flavian, Patriarch of Constantinople, in June 449 in anticipation of the 4th Ecumenical Council held at Chalcedon in 451. The question at issue was how Jesus could combine both divinity and humanity in one person.

[4] David Friedrich Strauss (1808-1874) was a lecturer at Tubingen University when, at the age of just 27, he wrote his *Leben Jesu* in 1835. It was a long and scholarly book, but a personal disaster. He was dismissed from his post and banished from academia. The book went through many editions and George Eliot made the first English translation.

[5] Albert Schweitzer (1875-1965) documented the Quest in his book *From Reimarus to Wrede*, written in 1906, only a few years before he abandoned theology for medicine. Hermann Reimarus (1694-1768), whom Schweitzer credits with launching the Quest, very wisely kept his thoughts to himself. It is only the English edition of Schweitzer's book, published by the SCM Press, that is known as *The Quest for the Historical Jesus*.

[6] *Pericope* (pronounced per-ik-kop-ee) is a Greek word meaning "a section", literally a unit that has been cut around. In Biblical Theology it has now become the technical term for a paragraph, or unit, or story in the Synoptic Gospels. Where John's Gospel is more or less seamless, the Synoptic Gospels are very bitty. These bits are the *pericope*.

[7] The word "paradigm" has only recently been introduced into Biblical studies. Its Greek derivation means, literally, "to show side by side". So a paradigm is a theory or conceptual framework, a way of looking at things. The Four Document Theory, although never described as such, is itself a paradigm. And so, too, is the new theory that has replaced it.

[8] Austin Farrer, at the time Chaplain of Trinity College, was the most original New Testament scholar in Oxford in the late 1950s. He lectured brilliantly and eccentrically at 12 noon on a Saturday morning to an audience of two or three. He was poorly regarded by many for changing his views from book to book, but well and affectionately regarded as a preacher. Michael Goulder dedicated his own first book (*Type and History in Acts*, 1964) to him: *Doctissimo Doctori. Scribamus spoliis, ille magister erat.* The article, "Dispensing with Q", was one in a collection of essays by different authors, published under the title *Studies in the Gospels*. Farrer wrote, "In postulating Q we are postulating the unique and the unevidenced". Quite so!

[9] Michael Goulder's name will recur throughout this Handbook and a separate chapter at the end pays tribute to him and lists his many books.

[10] Scribes could be very distinguished people, like Ezra ben Seraiah (Ezra 7. 6-10) and Jesus ben Sirah, the author of Ecclesiasticus in the Apocrypha (Ecclus 38.24 - 39.11). But most did not aspire to greatness and in the time of Jesus lived by teaching and copying Scripture. In small synagogues they could be required to fill other roles as well. Michael Goulder, whose first chapter in *Midrash and Lection in Matthew* explains the Scribe's role in great detail, quotes an example which will resonate with many a churchwarden seeking a new incumbent: "The people of Simonias asked the patriarch Judah to give them a man who could serve them as preacher, judge, Hazzan, sopher (Scribe), teacher of the law and whatever else they needed; and he sent them Levi ben-Sisi". It is a long time ago now, but I hope that they were not disappointed!

Table of Synoptic Parallels

		Mark	Matthew	Luke
1	John the Baptist	1. 1-11	3. 1-7	3. 1-22
2	The Temptation of Jesus	1. 12-13	4. 1-11	4. 1-13
3	The Preaching of Jesus	1. 14-15	4. 12-17	4. 14-15
4	The Call of the Disciples	1. 16-20	4. 18-22	
5	Casting out an evil spirit at Capernaum	1. 21-28		4. 31-37
6	The healing of Simon's mother-in-law	1. 29-31		4. 38-39
7	A first summary of Jesus' healing ministry	1. 32-34		4. 40-41
8	At prayer in a lonely spot	1. 35-39	4. 23-25	4. 42-44
9	The healing of a leper	1. 40-45	8. 1-4	5. 12-16
10	The healing of a paralysed man	2. 1-12	9. 1-8	5. 17-26
11	Jesus eats with tax gatherers	2. 13-17	9. 9-13	5. 27-32
12	Should the disciples fast?	2. 18-22	9. 14-17	5. 33-39
13	Plucking ears of corn on the Sabbath	2. 23-28	12. 1-8	6. 1-5
14	Healing a man with a withered arm	3. 1-6	12. 9-14	6. 6-11
15	A second summary of Jesus' healing ministry	3. 7-12	12. 15-21	6. 17-19
16	The Call of the Twelve	3. 13-19		6. 12-16
17	Is Jesus out of his mind?	3. 20-22	12. 22-24	
18	"He is possessed by Beelzebub"	3. 23-30	12. 25-37	
19	His mothers and brothers arrive	3. 31-35	12. 46-50	
20	The parable of the Sower	4. 1-20	13. 1-23	8. 4-15
21	The parable of the Lamp	4. 21-23		8. 16-17

		Mark	Matthew	Luke
22	The parable of the Measure	4. 24-25		
23	The parable of the Seed growing secretly	4. 26-29		
24	The parable of the Mustard Seed	4. 30-32	13. 31-32	
25	Jesus taught in parables	4. 33-34	13. 34-35	
26	Jesus stills the storm	4. 35-41		8. 22-25
27	The healing of the Gerasene demoniac	5. 1-20		8. 26-39
28	The healing of Jairus' daughter	5. 21-43		8. 40-56
29	Jesus is rejected in his home town	6. 1-6	13. 53-58	
30	Jesus sends out the disciples in pairs	6. 7-13		9. 1-6
31	Herod beheads John the Baptist	6. 14-29	14. 1-12	9. 7-9
32	The feeding of the five thousand	6. 30-44	14. 13-21	9. 10-17
33	Jesus walks on the lake	6. 45-52	14. 22-33	
34	A third summary of Jesus' healing ministry	6. 53-56	14. 34-36	
35	Jesus criticises Pharisaic traditions	7. 1-15	15. 1-14	
36	What really brings defilement	7. 16-23	15. 15-20	
37	The healing of a Gentile woman's child	7. 24-30	15. 21-28	
38	The healing of a deaf mute	7. 31-37	15. 29-31	
39	The feeding of the four thousand	8. 1-10	15. 32-39	
40	The Pharisees request a miracle	8. 11-13	16. 1-4	

		Mark	Matthew	Luke
41	The significance of the feeding miracles	8. 14-21	16. 5-12	
42	The healing of a blind man	8. 22-26		
43	Jesus' true identity and first prediction of the Passion	8. 27-33	16. 13-23	9. 18-22
44	What discipleship implies	8.34 – 9.1	16. 24-28	9. 23-27
45	The Transfiguration	9. 2-13	17. 1-13	9. 28-36
46	Jesus heals an epileptic child	9. 14-29	17. 14-21	9. 37-42
47	The second prediction of the Passion	9. 30-32	17. 22-23	9. 43-45
48	Who is the greatest?	9. 33-37	18. 1-5	9. 46-48
49	The man driving out devils	9. 38-41		9. 49-50
50	The cost of discipleship	9. 42-50	18. 6-9	
51	Marriage and divorce	10. 1-12	19. 1-12	
52	Children are brought to Jesus	10. 13-16	19. 13-15	18. 15-17
53	The rich young man	10. 17-31	19. 16-30	18. 18-30
54	The third prediction of the Passion	10. 32-34	20. 17-19	18. 31-34
55	James and John ask for positions of privilege	10. 35-45	20. 20-28	
56	The healing of blind Bartimaeus	10. 46-52	20. 29-34	18. 35-43
57	Jesus enters Jerusalem	11. 1-11	21. 1-17	19. 28-46
58	Jesus curses the fig tree	11. 12-14	21. 18-19	
59	Jesus ejects the traders from the temple	11. 15-19		19. 47-48
60	The withered fig tree and the power of prayer	11. 20-26	21. 20-22	
61	Jesus' authority is challenged	11. 27-33	21. 23-27	20. 1-8

		Mark	*Matthew*	*Luke*
62	The parable of the Vineyard	12. 1-12	21. 33-46	20. 9-19
63	Paying tribute to Caesar	12. 13-17	22. 15-22	20. 20-26
64	About the resurrection of the dead	12. 18-27	22. 23-33	20. 27-40
65	The great commandment	12. 28-34	22. 34-40	
66	About David's son	12. 35-37	22. 41-46	20. 41-44
67	"Beware of the Scribes"	12. 38-40	23. 1-39	20. 45-47
68	The widow's two tiny coins	12. 41-44		21. 1-4
69	The Passover Discourse	13	24. 1-44	21. 5-38
70	The Conspiracy	14. 1-2	26. 1-5	22. 1-2
71	The Anointing at Bethany	14. 3-9	26. 6-13	
72	Judas goes to the Chief Priests	14. 10-11	26. 14-16	22. 3-6
73	The preparation of the Passover Meal	14. 12-16	26. 17-19	22. 7-13
74	The Last Supper	14. 17-25	26. 20-29	22. 14-20
75	"You will all fall from your faith"	14. 26-31	26. 30-35	22.39
76	Gethsemane	14. 32-42	26. 36-46	20. 40-46
77	Jesus is arrested	14. 43-52	26. 47-56	22. 47-53
78	Jesus is tried at the High Priest's house	14. 53-65	26. 57-68	
79	Peter's Denial	14. 66-72	26. 69-75	22. 54-62
80	The Trial before Pilate	15. 1-15	27. 1-26	23. 1-25
81	Jesus is mocked	15. 16-20	27. 27-31	
82	The Crucifixion	15. 21-41	27. 32-54	23. 26-49
83	The Deposition and Burial	15. 42-47	27. 55-61	23. 50-56
84	The Empty Tomb	16. 1-8	28. 1-10	24. 1-12

Notes:

Mark's Gospel is shown in its entirety. The comparable passages in Matthew and Luke are only shown when they occur *in the same order* as in Mark. So the fact that no reference is given in the Matthew and Luke columns does not imply that they have left out the Markan passage altogether. They may just have included it elsewhere, out of order, or they may have re-written the text beyond immediate recognition.

There is, however, one big gap in the Lukan column (sections 33-42). This is known as the Great Omission. Luke leaves out Mark 6.45 – 8.26, the equivalent of some two whole chapters. But, in practice, while Matthew omits almost nothing in Mark, Luke, with this exception, also leaves out relatively little. The two so-called Lesser Omissions are very much shorter (Mark 3. 20-35 and 4. 26-34)

Both Matthew and Luke are much longer Gospels than Mark's. So they obviously have a lot of extra material. Much of Matthew's extra material is found in the discourses, which are a feature of his Gospel. Chapters 5 - 7, 10, 13, 18 and 24 - 25 are his discourses for the Jewish festivals of Pentecost, New Year, Tabernacles, Hanukkah and Passover. By contrast Luke has mostly confined his extra material to the so-called Lukan Journey (9.51 – 18.14) in which Jesus travels from Galilee to Jerusalem with the disciples, as he teaches them about the Christian life. Matthew and Luke also both have Birth and Post-Resurrection Narratives, where Mark has nothing. All of this will be explained in the chapters that follow.

In listing the *pericope* I have used the New English Bible Library edition, which disregards the traditional division of the text into separate verses. Readers working from other translations may therefore find their division of the text varies slightly from mine.

THE GOSPEL ACCORDING TO MARK[1]

Mark's is by some measure the shortest of the Synoptic Gospels. It has sixteen chapters against twenty-eight in Matthew and twenty-four in Luke, or thirty-five pages in the New English Bible Library Edition, against fifty-four for Matthew and fifty-eight for Luke. The reason for this may not just be that Mark had less to say, although he may have done, but that he intended his Gospel to provide lections in Christian synagogues for only seven months of the year - from Jewish New Year (1st Tishri), in early October, to Passover or Easter (15th Nisan), some time in April. This is explained in the chapter on the Christian Lectionary.

An Outline of Mark's Gospel

Printed and read as we read them in church today, it is very difficult for congregations to have any sense of the overall shape of a Gospel. So no one, unless they attend a theatre performance, ever hears Mark's Gospel read from beginning to end. A brief outline of its content (and omissions) may therefore be helpful.

There is, first of all, no Birth Narrative. For Mark the Gospel of Jesus Christ begins with the preaching of John the Baptist, in fulfilment of Scripture. The point may seem academic to some, but it is important. To understand Mark's perspective, we have to rid our minds of the whole idea of incarnation and other subsequent church doctrines. For him, Jesus was a man upon whom God's Spirit had descended.

This brief introduction leads immediately into a ministry of hectic activity. One story follows another in rapid succession until we reach chapter 4, which is the first landmark. This is a little book of parables (the Sower, the Lamp, the Measure, the Seed growing secretly, and the Mustard Seed). The discourse has a formal conclusion: "With many such parables he would give them his message..." (Mark 4.33). These, with the Vineyard (Mark 12. 1-12) and the Householder (Mark 13. 33-37), are very much in the style of rabbinic parables, with a high allegorical score. But there are far fewer parables than in

Matthew and Luke and, although Mark writes of "many such parables", he only includes these seven. The miracle stories far outnumber them.

Most commentators have argued that Mark 8. 27-33 is the next important landmark, and it is indeed a watershed inasmuch as the disciples at last stumble upon the identity of Jesus. There are also the first references to the Passion and there is a change of mood, which suddenly becomes more sombre. Mark 10.32 ("They were on the road, going up to Jerusalem....") also seems to mark a further development. But the very fact that we alight on these verses, looking for seams, illustrates how few real seams there are. From the beginning until very much further on, Mark's Gospel can seem like a succession of short, unrelated units, which just follow on, one after another. It appears to have very little structure.

The entry of Jesus into Jerusalem (Mark 11. 1-11) is a very well known story today and will be familiar to many people through its commemoration on Palm Sunday. But there is nothing in the text to suggest its particular importance. It is only one story in a succession of stories and is given no greater emphasis than any other. This is also true of Mark's account of the Last Supper (Mark 14. 17-25), which is embedded in the Passion Narrative.

Mark 13, however, is a real landmark. It is a second discourse, longer than the earlier one in chapter 4, and it introduces the Passion Narrative. Although seemingly irrelevant to us (we no longer look for an imminent end to the world) it is absolutely central to Mark's purpose. It is a Passover Discourse (the Second Coming of Jesus was expected at Passover) and it served to address the church as it gathered to keep the annual vigil commemorating Jesus' death. It ends, "Be alert, be wakeful....for you do not know when the master of the house is coming. Evening or midnight, cock-crow or early dawn – if he comes suddenly he must not find you asleep" (Mark 13. 33-37). So Mark's church are reminded that this year may be the year of the Lord's return. They must be ready.

This discourse introduces the Passion Narrative, which is analysed in detail in a separate chapter. But the events of the next twenty-four hours occupy a fifth of Mark's Gospel (a third, if the discourse in chapter 13 is included). And his is undoubtedly the most harrowing narrative of the four. Jesus is silent throughout and there is no relief of any sort. The story is relentlessly heartbreaking and finds its saddest expression in the text from Psalm 22, "My God, my God, why have you forsaken me", which Jesus makes his own. It was not a sentiment with which either Luke or John identified and, as we shall see, they left it out.

Finally, it is important to notice where Mark's Gospel ends, at Mark 16.8. There are no resurrection appearances. The verses that follow (Mark 16. 9-20) are only found in one of the three oldest manuscripts of the New Testament and cannot have been part of the original text. What they do is to summarize the resurrection appearance stories found in the *other* Gospels, and were presumably added by an early copyist who felt that Mark 16.8 represented a very dire ending: The women "went out and ran away from the tomb, beside themselves with terror. They said nothing to anybody, because they were afraid." It is easy to understand his point of view, but it was not Mark's.

One of the oldest debates in the many commentaries on Mark's Gospel is whether he really intended to finish his Gospel like this, but it seems very probable that he did. Mark's overview of the story of Jesus does not require a resurrection appearance because it reaches its natural end with the verdict of the Roman centurion: "Truly this man was a Son of God" (Mark 15.39). Mark had begun his Gospel by telling us that Jesus was the Son of God, and he ends with the independent testimony of an objective witness that it was so. All had by then been revealed and attested. Mark does not look, or need, to prove anything further. The proof of Jesus' claim to be the Son of God is to be found in the Passion Narrative.

So Mark's final paragraphs (Mark 15.40 – 16.8) are really a postscript. The burial of Jesus at 6.00 pm brings the Easter vigil to an end. The church had gathered on the Mount of Olives on the Thursday afternoon for the Passover Discourse and now, just over a day later, as Easter Saturday begins, breaks up to go home. This had not been the year of the Lord's Return and they would gather again next year.

Mark's is the only Gospel to divide the Passion Narrative into three-hour watches like this and, presumably, was the only one of the four to have been used for a Vigil. It must therefore have been written before AD 70, when Jerusalem was destroyed by Roman armies. By implication, too, Matthew's Gospel was probably written after this date, when the sites were no longer there to visit.

The Messianic Secret

We come now to Mark's *understanding* of the story he told. He shared with Matthew and Luke a belief that the ministry of Jesus heralded the coming of God's kingdom and was a foretaste of it. Jesus himself was the Son of God (the Messiah, or Messiah designate). But in human terms his ministry was a failure. Everything continued as before. The church, however, expected his early return and vindication, and the dawn of a new age. The role of disciples in these circumstances was to cherish his memory, remain faithful to his teaching, and await his return. This, broadly, is the view of all three Synoptic Gospels.

Each evangelist, however, gave the story a different emphasis and had his own perspective on it. Mark's was that Jesus, as the Son of God, was *predestined* to die. The story of his life was scripted. It could never have turned out otherwise than it did, and consequently the truth about Jesus' status and destiny had to be kept secret lest, through public knowledge, it never came to be fulfilled. For if people had known that Jesus was the Messiah, they might have accepted him, and the outcome of his life would then have been very different. So Jesus himself *must* have refused to disclose his identity and in various ways ensured that the Secret was not publicly revealed until his trial. He was the Son of God *incognito*. This was Mark's conclusion.

Since it is inconceivable that Jesus was in fact deliberately secretive, we must ask why Mark should represent him as such, and the probable answer becomes clearer when we put ourselves in his position. In telling the story of Jesus, he had to ask himself why Jesus, the Son of God, was rejected and crucified. It cannot have been because there was any doubt as to his identity and status. It must, therefore, have been because

God intended it and, in the Old Testament, he found scriptural confirmation of this. So the idea of the Messianic Secret, as Biblical scholars now call it, became central to Mark's understanding of the story of Jesus. As a matter of historical fact he must surely have been mistaken, but as a literary device it gives his account of the Passion, in particular, a unique poignancy. And like DNA in human cells, the Secret can be found in almost every unit of Mark's Gospel.

The Scriptures which underlie the Secret

The best place to begin is probably Mark 4. 10-12, where the Secret is explained. Jesus says: "To you [the disciples] the *secret* of the kingdom of God has been given; but to those who are outside everything comes by way of parables, so that (as Scripture says) they may look and look, but see nothing; they may hear and hear, but understand nothing; otherwise they might turn to God and be forgiven." The reference is to Isaiah 6. 9-10. Did Jesus, then, really teach in parables to confuse people? Indisputably, Mark thought so. Did Jesus not wish people to repent and be forgiven? Not in Mark's view.

Another Old Testament text that was almost certainly in Mark's mind was Daniel 12. 8-13. The Book of Daniel as a whole was hugely important in shaping the church's understanding of the story of Jesus and belongs to a style of writing known as Apocalyptic[3]. Mark, Matthew, and Luke all believed, albeit with slightly different emphases, that the life of Jesus had set the drama of the End of the World in motion. They describe the process in detail in their Passover Discourses (Mark 13; Matthew 24 - 25; Luke 21. 5-end) and expected it to happen at any time. Paul, too, believed that it would happen within his own lifetime (1 Corinthians 15. 51-57).

The Book of Daniel divides into two parts. It begins in, chapters 1 – 6, with some stirring stories, set during the period of the Exile (586–c.520 BC), to encourage bravery in the face of persecution. Then, in chapters 7 -12, there follows a series of visions which predict the future course of history and describe how the End of the World will come. Returning, then, to Daniel 12. 8-13, which prompted this digression, Daniel asks "the man clothed in linen", "What will the issue of these things be?" He replied, "Go your way, Daniel, *for the words are kept secret and sealed till the end of time*"(Daniel 12. 8-9). Here, then, was further confirmation of Mark's basic presumption and, with this in mind, we are in a position to follow Mark's text from beginning to end.

The Secret progressively revealed

The opening section (Mark 1. 1-13) is obviously critical. Mark introduces his Gospel with these words: "Here begins the Gospel of Jesus Christ, *the Son of God*". This is the Secret and, if Mark's church is to understand the story of Jesus, they need to know this. It is the essential clue.

The Secret is confirmed to Jesus himself at his baptism. The voice from heaven tells him (*and him alone*): "Thou art my Son, my Beloved; on thee my favour rests" (Mark 1.11). Mark's readers must keep this in mind at all times. It is the Secret which explains everything.

Also in the know are the unclean spirits (Mark 1. 21-28). One shrieks, "I know who you are – the Holy One of God". Jesus first rebukes the spirit, "Be silent" (lest everyone else find out), and then exorcises it to the astonishment of onlookers who, not knowing the Secret, are completely baffled, and speculate endlessly. As Mark tells the story, healings and exorcisms were a prominent feature of Jesus' ministry, "but he would not let the devils speak, because they knew who he was" and must not be allowed to say (Mark 1.34). In the same way, those who are healed are sworn to silence (Mark 1. 44-45).

So the mystery deepens. People think that Jesus must be John the Baptist, or Elijah, or another of "the old prophets" (Mark 6. 14-16). Herod concludes (wrongly, of course) that Jesus is "John, whom I beheaded, returned to life". But how could he know? There are clues for the discerning, but even the disciples overlook them. They are completely dumbfounded at the Feeding of the Five Thousand (Mark 6. 30-44) and, again, when Jesus walks on the water (Mark 6. 45-52). As Mark succinctly puts it, "their minds were closed". The evidence was to hand, but the conclusion escaped them.

The two feeding miracles seem to have been particularly significant to Mark (Mark 6. 11-21). The Pharisees ask Jesus for

29

a "sign from heaven". They want to know the Secret, too, but are a very long way from finding out. But the disciples themselves have still some way to go. Jesus says to them, "Why do you talk about having no bread? Have you no inkling yet? Do you still not understand? Are your minds closed? You have eyes: can you not see? You have ears: can you not hear? Have you forgotten?" (Mark 8. 17-21). We can all answer these rhetorical questions on behalf of the disciples (five Noes and one Yes), but the fact that Mark has Jesus ask the question *six* times illustrates the importance which he attaches to understanding the Secret. They are close to understanding (they have all the evidence), but the truth about Jesus still eludes them.

Mark 8. 27-33 (the so-called watershed) can now also be seen as a *theological* landmark, if not a real division in the text, for it is the moment at which the disciples at last discover the Secret. "You are the Messiah", Peter exclaims on their behalf, but they, too, are now sworn to secrecy. Jesus tells them about his forthcoming Passion and when Peter protests at this, he is rebuked. The Passion is *God's* plan, and they must not frustrate it, as Satan would wish them to do.

The climax of the Gospel comes at the trial of Jesus, when the High Priest at last also elicits the Secret. He confronts Jesus face to face and asks him, "Are you the Messiah, the Son of the Blessed one?" Jesus replies, "I am; and you will see the Son of Man [that is, Jesus himself] seated on the right hand of God and coming with the clouds of heaven" (Mark 14. 61-64). His reply is unambiguous and unequivocal. But, for the enemies of Jesus, it is now too late. The Passion of Jesus is under way and cannot be halted. The need for secrecy is past. For the present, he is their prisoner, but very shortly he will return as their judge.

All of this is anticipated in Mark's description of the events that precede his trial. Jesus had said at the Last Supper, "The Son of Man is going the way *appointed for him in the Scriptures*" (Mark 14.21), and again at his arrest: "Day after day I was within your reach as I taught in the temple, and you did not lay hands on me. *But let the Scriptures be fulfilled*" (Mark 14.49). And so they were, Psalm 22 in particular. In Mark's view, they *had* to be fulfilled. It was not a matter of chance. It was God's plan *from the beginning*.

In many ways Mark's Passion Narrative is the most moving of the four. As we follow it, we hope in our heart of hearts that something may avert the tragedy we fear. But it is no good hoping. The whole story has been scripted by God, and everyone has been given their part to play. Pity those, like Judas, who have been assigned the wrong parts. It is not really their fault. They are just, helplessly, playing out the roles that have been allocated to them. Even the disciples, for all their protestations of loyalty, abandon him (Mark 14. 30-31). That is just how it had to be. So every last chance slips by, while Jesus himself becomes increasingly silent. It is a relentless story, wonderfully told. All things are possible to God, and this is what he wills (Mark 14.36 and 14.50).

Confirmation of the Secret comes when the Roman Centurion, a dispassionate observer who knew nothing about Jesus except what he had seen during his crucifixion and death, concludes, "Truly this man was a Son of God" (Mark 15.39). There is then nothing further to add or do, except to wait.

Mark's story was told. But not everyone, however loyal, would follow him all the way and we shall see in the following sections how two of his most faithful followers, Matthew and Luke, reinterpreted the story he had bequeathed them.

---

[1] The New English Bible was the first English translation to leave out the *St* in referring to each of the New Testament authors. The translators did this because, although it had become traditional to include it, it does not actually occur in any of the earliest manuscripts. I prefer to follow their example.

[2] The chapters and verses that we use today post-date the Gospels by many centuries and are irrelevant except as a convenient way of identifying an individual text.

[3] The name derives from the Greek word *apokalupto. Kalupto* means "to hide", and *apokalupto* means "to reveal". So an *apokalupsis* is "a revelation". We use the word today to refer specifically to a revelation of what will happen at the End of the World, so that the last book in the New Testament is actually called the Revelation (correctly *Apocalypse*) of John.

Mark's Gospel and the Messianic Secret

1.1	The title: Jesus is the Son of God.	The reader is told the Secret.
1. 2-13	The Baptism of Jesus.	Jesus is told the Secret.
1.14 - 3.35	Jesus' ministry begins and the Twelve Disciples are chosen.	The unclean spirits are silenced and the Secret kept.
4. 1-34	A Discourse for Tabernacles: A Book of Harvest Parables in the Rabbinic style.	Parables serve to mislead ordinary people, but are explained privately to the disciples.
4.35 - 8.26	The ministry of Jesus continues. The Mission of the Twelve and its outcome.	The disciples are still unable to explain the significance of the Feeding of the Five Thousand and other miracles.
8.27 - 10.31	Jesus confides in his disciples at Caesarea Philippi. The first predictions of the Passion.	The disciples discover the Secret, confirmed by Moses and Elijah at the Transfiguration.
10.32 - 12.44	The journey to Jerusalem amidst growing conflict.	The Chief Priests, Scribes and Pharisees puzzle over the authority and identity of Jesus.
13	The Passover Discourse and prophecies about the return of Jesus at the end of the world.	Jesus prepares his disciples for the Passover Vigil. Will this be the year in which he returns?
14.1 - 15.38	The Passion Narrative	The true identity of Jesus is revealed to all at his trial. The High Priest asks him, "Are you the Messiah?" and Jesus replies, "I am".

15.39	The verdict of an independent and dispassionate witness	The centurion concludes: "Truly this man was a Son of God".
15.40 - 16.8	Postscript: The burial and empty tomb.	The disciples are still dumbfounded, but the story is now complete.

As explained on page 26, Mark 16. 9-20 is not part of the original text and has been left out accordingly.

THE GOSPEL ACCORDING TO MATTHEW

Matthew's Gospel stands first in the New Testament and was probably the preferred Gospel in most Jewish Christian congregations[1]. It is essentially a re-write or expansion of Mark's Gospel and, at twenty-eight chapters, is very considerably longer. Very little of Mark is omitted and some of the few stories which appear at first sight to have been left out, prove in practice to have been included after all. They have just been re-written beyond immediate recognition. So, for example, Mark's parable of the Seed growing secretly (Mark 4. 26-29) becomes Matthew's parable of the Wheat and the Tares (Matthew 13. 24-30). And not only does Matthew include all this Markan material, but much of it is copied, literally. There is a word for word correspondence and the stories are also, for the most part, in the Markan order.

A Christian Scribe

We know nothing of Matthew himself except what we can learn about him from his own Gospel, but the very fact of his relying so heavily upon Mark proves conclusively that he cannot have been Matthew the disciple. If he had had his own recollection of the story he tells, he would have had no need of a secondary source.

One of the incidental details which Michael Goulder's brilliant study of Matthew[2] has revealed is his ambivalent attitude towards Scribes. In Mark's Gospel the Scribes and Pharisees are, without exception, the bitter opponents of Jesus. Nothing good can be said about them. All but two references in Mark are hostile. But Matthew only partly follows Mark in this. The Scribes were, indeed, largely responsible for the death of Jesus. There can be no disagreement about that. But of Mark's nineteen hostile references to Scribes only six are retained. Another six are dropped and a further six are glossed, where they are replaced by "the Pharisees", or "the elders of the people". But most revealing of all is Matthew's re-write of Mark 1.22 at Matthew 7.29 (the end of the Sermon on the

Mount). Mark has: "The people were astounded at his teaching, for unlike the Scribes, he taught with a note of authority." Matthew has: "The people were astounded at his teaching; unlike *their* Scribes, he taught with a note of authority." Matthew has added a "their", we must assume, to contrast "their" Scribes (the ones who were so hostile to Jesus) with "our" Scribes (followers of Jesus and members of the church). *They* can be thoroughly useful people in writing Christian Scripture.

Confirmation of this comes at Matthew 13. 51-52, a very positive reference to Scribes: "When, therefore, a Scribe has become a disciple, he is like a householder who can produce from his store both the new and the old."[3] These verses come at the end of the third discourse (of which more later) and their meaning has never been clear, although the verses are easily translated. But perhaps Matthew thought of *himself* as a "Scribe who has become a disciple". He is, after all, doing the work of a Scribe in re-writing Mark. And so, on this reading, Mark is "the old" (the material he has faithfully copied) while his own amplification and expansion of Mark is "the new".

In Matthew 13 he is re-writing Mark's first discourse (Mark 4. 1-34). The parable of the Mustard-seed, then, would represent "the old" (he has found it at Mark 4. 30-32 and reproduces it at Matthew 13. 31-32), while the parables of the Buried Treasure and the Pearl of Great Price (Matthew 13. 44-46) are "the new". He has written them himself. But he did not make them up. He found his inspiration for them in the little parable of the Lamp in Mark 4.22 ("For nothing is hidden unless it is to be disclosed, and nothing put under cover unless it is to come into the open."). For what is the Gospel but "hidden treasure" (Mark 10. 20-21)? To Christian Scribes like Matthew, who studied their chosen text (Mark) with such immense and loving care, parables write themselves. And the parable of the Pearl of Great Price? It makes a pair with the Buried Treasure – the treasures of land and sea.

Matthew then was a Christian Scribe ("a Scribe Discipled" as Michael Goulder puts it). He found inspiration, of course, in the Old Testament as well, as any Jewish Christian would, and was at pains to realign Mark with Jewish tradition, where Mark portrays Jesus as being overly radical (as it seemed to Matthew). But it is done very subtly, just clarifying what Matthew assumed to have been a misunderstanding or over-statement. Matthew's loyalty to Mark is immense.

Matthew's Five Discourses

But the principal problem with Mark's Gospel, in Matthew's view, was that it was too short. A subsequent chapter will discuss the Christian Lectionary in greater detail, but if Mark's Gospel was intended to provide lections from Jewish New Year to Passover (say, October to April), what were they to read for the rest of the year (from May to September)? Here was an urgent practical need. And if Mark 4 and Mark 13 had provided his church with readings for the festivals of Tabernacles and Passover, what were they to read at Pentecost, New Year and Hanukkah? This was work for a Christian Scribe.

Matthew's Gospel contains five discourses (chapters 5 - 7, 10, 13, 18, and 24 - 25) of which the third and the last are essentially Mark's, although expanded. These are big blocks of material and stand out from the text because Matthew ends each of them with an identical formula, which translated literally reads: "And it came to pass that when Jesus had finished these words (instructions, parables)...." (nine words in Greek). These discourses were intended to provide readings for the five principal Jewish festivals. Their themes are appropriate and they fall in the right place. They are where we would expect them to be. So the discourses can be spread across the Jewish Year as follows:

Matthew 5 - 7	The Sermon on the Mount	Pentecost
Matthew 9.35 - 11.1	Jesus commissions the disciples	New Year
Matthew 13. 1-52	A book of harvest parables	Tabernacles
Matthew 18	The care of the church	Hanukkah
Matthew 24 - 25	The Lord's Return	Passover

The Sermon on the Mount is much the best known of these discourses and there is a separate chapter in which it is analysed in greater detail. But the Jewish theme for Pentecost was a celebration of the Law, and Matthew's discourse therefore has Jesus ascend a mountain, like Moses, to reinterpret the Law and to set out a new Ten Commandments for Christians.

The theme of Jewish New Year is the joyful inauguration of God's kingdom and his judgement on those who do not welcome it, or are not prepared for it. Jesus' own ministry of preaching and healing was itself a sign that this new dawn was about to break and in his New Year discourse Matthew has Jesus extend this ministry to his disciples. They are to go out into the towns and villages of Israel, healing and preaching. And they must be prepared for conflict, as Matthew's own experience as a Christian Jew will have confirmed. New Year is a time of judgement.

Tabernacles, which falls in the autumn, was originally a harvest thanksgiving and Matthew follows Mark and amplifies his little book of harvest parables (Mark 4). The festival also later became a commemoration of the founding of the temple, which Solomon had consecrated at Tabernacles (1 Kings 8). Solomon was famous for his wisdom. "He uttered three thousand parables and discoursed of trees, of beasts and birds, of reptiles and fishes. Men of all races came to listen to the wisdom of Solomon." (1 Kings 4. 31-34). Matthew sees Solomon as "a type" of Jesus. "The Queen of the South came from the ends of the earth to hear the wisdom of Solomon; and what is here is greater than Solomon" (Matthew 12.42). So Jesus is not only another Moses. He is another Solomon as well, and in each case greater than his forerunner.

Hanukkah is another festival of the temple. Where Tabernacles celebrates its founding, Hanukkah celebrates its rededication. 2 Maccabees 2 tells the story of how Jeremiah hid the "the tent, the ark, and the incense altar" from Solomon's temple in a cave, just before this first temple was destroyed in 586 BC. A second temple was built by the exiles, when they returned from Babylon, but this, too, was destroyed and desecrated by Antiochus Epiphanes in 170 BC. It led, however, to the Maccabean revolt, the rededication of the third temple amidst much pomp, and the return of the Shekinah, the Glory

Cloud, which had led Moses through the Sinai desert and had been seen to leave the first temple on its destruction. As Hanukkah approaches, therefore, Matthew's church first read the story of the Transfiguration (Matthew 17. 1-17), when the Shekinah is seen to rest upon Jesus, and then listened to his discourse for Hanukkah (Matthew 18), which sets out the rules by which the disciples are to govern the church.

Matthew's final discourse, for Passover (Matthew 24-25), is an expansion of Mark's (Mark 13) and prepares his congregation, on the eve of their commemoration of Jesus' Passion, for his possible return.

The Table of Descent

Matthew begins his Gospel with a Table of Descent (Matthew 1. 1-17). It gives us an interesting insight into the way in which he thought. On a completely straightforward view of the matter, Matthew is telling us, for our interest, who Jesus' paternal grandfather, great grandfather, and so forth, were. It is an odd thing to do because he is also about to tell us that Jesus was not actually related to Joseph, his supposed father, after all. But he leaves a clue as to his meaning in adding up the generations for us: 14 + 14 + 14 (= 42) (Matthew 1.17).

The idea of beginning in this way was very probably suggested by the Old Testament. Genesis has many Tables of Descent (in chapters 5, 10, 11, 25 and 36, to quote only the longest). So, too, does the Chronicler, who began Israel's history with eight whole chapters of genealogies (1 Chronicles 1-8). But Matthew is going to do something different. Following Daniel 9. 24-27[4], he is going to *count* in generations, with each generation representing a week. So there have been six weeks of weeks since the days of Abraham (that is, 42 generations) and we are now therefore entering the week of the Messiah, God's Sabbath, the seventh week of weeks, and the end of history. As Jesus himself was to announce, "The kingdom of heaven is at hand" (Matthew 4.17). The end of the ages is upon us and the time of fulfilment has come. It is a stirring beginning.

Matthew's Parables

There are separate chapters on the Synoptic Parables and Miracles, and on the Birth and Passion Narratives. To avoid duplication, therefore, this chapter has to be read in conjunction with these. And, because of their inherent interest, there are also separate chapters on the Sermon on the Mount, and on the Lord's Prayer, which is found within it. But, because of their sheer quantity and importance, I have added this further section on Matthew's parables. He himself was not averse to duplication, if it made an important point more clearly and more forcefully.

Today, parables are the most popular aspect of Jesus' teaching and they are regularly read in church and taught in schools. Stories, after all, are memorable and the best known parables are very well known indeed. But many people may not realise that parables are mostly confined to Matthew's and Luke's Gospels. Mark has seven (but five are very short). John and Paul have none at all, nor probably saw the need for any. But Matthew and Luke have a great many, and when we explore how Matthew has bulked up Mark's Gospel, it is not miracle stories that he has added but parables. In fact many of Mark's miracle stories are shortened as, for example, the story of the Gerasene Demoniac (Mark 5. 1-20; Matthew 8. 28-34). Matthew would not leave anything in Mark out, but, as a Christian Scribe, no doubt bore his congregation in mind and shortened or glossed as he thought appropriate. The effect is to change the balance of Jesus' ministry. Mark's Gospel has the single book of parables (Mark 4) but is otherwise dominated by miracles and disputes. Matthew includes these, but the many parables which he introduces into his other discourses give his Gospel greater contemporary interest. It comes across as more positive. Preachers never know what to say about miracle stories, but parables are a gift.

So Jesus taught in parables, and perhaps told the parables which Mark re-tells. It has been noticed, however, that Matthew's and Luke's parables are very different from one another in both style and content. Matthew's are highly allegorical, with little or no incidental detail, tell the story of kings, deal in stereotypes, and have a very clear-cut message (a warning). Luke's parables are less allegorical, with incidental detail that makes the stories more interesting, are about ordinary people, and deal with different aspects of discipleship - prayer, money, and penitence, for example. But many scholars, wanting to represent *all* the parables as the parables of Jesus, are reluctant to accept the corollary which inevitably follows – that Matthew and Luke each wrote their own parables themselves. They were not just editors, who strung together the recollections of Jesus' contemporaries in a random order. They were creative authors, Scribes, as we have seen. But Matthew did not make his parables up; he found them in Scripture (and primarily in Mark).

The parable of the Talents (Matthew 25. 14-30) is a good example. It comes in the Passover Discourse. Matthew is midrashing Mark 13, where he finds the little parable of the Householder (Mark 13. 33-37), and he decides to amplify it by writing three parables which each take up one aspect of it. Mark says that the householder "put his servants in charge" of his house while he was away. So Matthew develops that in the third of his parables. Almost every detail of the story is allegorical – the householder is Jesus, his servants are the church, his capital is the Gospel, his going away is his death, his return is the Second Coming, and "your master's delight" is heaven. The black and white contrast is between the two servants who fulfil their trust, and the one who does not. There is no attempt to characterise them or make them interesting. The conversation which each has with his master on his return is repetitive. The scale is vast – a talent is a huge amount of money. The moral is characteristic ("Be warned!"), and the outcome is typically Matthaean (the unfaithful servant is thrown into hell). Matthew's story is not true to life (the punishment is grossly disproportionate), but the moral is everything. Luke's parables, as we shall see, are very different.

The Pre-eminent Gospel

We can see now why Matthew's Gospel replaced Mark's. It has everything that Mark's Gospel has, but much more. For although Matthew is faithful to Mark, the extra material which he has added alters the whole balance of the Gospel. Where

Mark's emphasis lay upon the Passion Narrative, Matthew also provides a memorable Birth Narrative. Where Mark has just two discourses, Matthew has five and, most memorable of all, the Sermon on the Mount. And Matthew has provided a fitting and triumphant conclusion to his Gospel in the Great Commission (Matthew 28. 16-20), where Mark's ends tentatively. Matthew includes the texts in which Mark explains the Messianic Secret, but its impact is diminished by his adding so many extra parables. He portrays Jesus positively, as a teacher of wisdom, greater even than Solomon, and not simply as a victim of God's providence. And (this was perhaps decisive in promoting Matthew's Gospel) he has a lesson for every week in the year, and not just for six months. Happily, however, Mark's Gospel has been treasured as well and, through our having his text before us, we can see how Matthew went to work and, as a Christian Scribe, amplified and expounded Mark's Gospel to his own congregation.

[1] We know this from Eusebius of Caesarea (*The History of the Church* Book 3, Chapter 27, and Book 5, Chapter 8).

[2] *Midrash and Lection in Matthew* by M.D.Goulder (SPCK 1974)

[3] For all its merits the New English Bible translation has annoying faults. It tends to paraphrase where there is no need to do so and particularly if the translators judge the meaning of a verse to be unclear. So in this verse they translate the word *Scribe* as "a teacher of the law" and a *disciple* as "a learner in the kingdom of heaven" (Matthew 13. 51-52). To bring clarity to the meaning of these two passages, I have corrected their translation.

[4] The passage is too long to quote in full, but it begins, "Seventy weeks are marked out for your people and your holy city...".

Matthew's Gospel in Outline

	Matthew	Mark
The Table of Descent and Birth Narrative	1 - 2	
John the Baptist, the temptation of Jesus, and call of the first disciples	3 - 4	1. 1-39
A discourse for Pentecost: The Sermon on the Mount	5 - 7	
The ministry of Jesus	8 - 9	1.40 - 2.22
A discourse for New Year: the Call and Commissioning of the Twelve	10 - 11.1	
The ministry of Jesus continues	11.2 - 12	2.23 - 3.35
A discourse for Tabernacles: a Book of Harvest Parables	13. 1-52	4. 1-34
The ministry of Jesus resumes	13.53 - 17	6 - 9.32
A discourse for Hanukkah: The Governance of the Church	18	
The ministry of Jesus concludes	19 - 23	10 - 12
A discourse for Passover: the Second Coming of Jesus	24 - 25	13
The Passion Narrative	26 - 27	14 - 15
The Empty Tomb and Great Commission.	28	16. 1-8

Note: Some Markan material is taken out of order and, to keep things simple, the correspondence is not then shown.

THE GOSPEL ACCORDING TO LUKE

Luke was not one of the Twelve Disciples and there is no immediate reason to doubt his authorship, either of the Gospel attributed to him, or of the Acts of the Apostles, which we can infer he also wrote (Acts 1.1). So, in all, Luke wrote more than a quarter of the whole New Testament, an immense achievement. There are also three references to him in other New Testament books, two in genuinely Pauline epistles (Colossians 4.14 and Philemon 24) and one in a much later Pastoral Epistle (2 Timothy 4.11).

However, the internal evidence of the Gospel itself makes an early date impossible. It is clear that Luke's Gospel was the third of the Synoptic Gospels to be written and post-dates both Mark and Matthew. There is also the evidence of Luke 6.22: "How blest you are when men hate you, when they *outlaw* you and insult you, and *ban your name* as infamous, because of the Son of Man". This seems a clear and specific reference to the Birkath-ha-Minim (ironically known as the Blessing of the Sectaries), which dates from around AD 85, by which *Christian* Jews were permanently and finally excluded from Orthodox Jewish synagogues. It means that Luke's Gospel cannot have been written much before AD 90.

Luke's Purpose in Writing

As regards Luke's aims and intentions in writing his Gospel, we have his own words on which to rely (Luke 1. 1-4). The problem lies in interpreting them. Because of their importance it is worth quoting the verses in full: "The author to Theophilus: *Many witnesses* have undertaken to draw up an account of the events that have happened among us, following the traditions handed down to us by the original eyewitnesses and servants of the Gospel. And so I in my turn, your Excellency, as one who has gone over the whole course of these events in detail, have decided to write *a connected narrative* for you, so as to give you authentic knowledge about the matters of which you have been *informed*."

So Luke is writing to Theophilus ("Lover of God"), which may refer to someone specific, but more probably to any Christian. Who, then, first of all, are the "many witnesses"? Although "many" may seem an exaggeration, this can only refer to Mark and Matthew. They were the only people to have done what Luke says ("drawn up an account of the events that have happened among us") and he quotes from them, occasionally word for word, but many, many times loosely. There are no other "lost" writings for which there is any evidence. What Luke is going to do is to conflate Mark and Matthew, and add some material of his own. They are his witnesses and principal texts.

What, next, of the "connected narrative"? Here the New English Bible translation is characteristically vague. What Luke proposes to do is to tell his story "in order". But what order? Chronological order might seem sensible, but there is no evidence for this. Luke generally follows Mark's order, but not exclusively. A more probable suggestion is that he has a liturgical order in mind. No church today wants two hymn books, and nor did Luke's church want two Gospels. So Luke would consolidate them and put his *pericope* (theirs and his own) in the order in which they would be read in church. For he, like Mark and Matthew, is providing a series of lections, in his case (as in Matthew's) for a whole year, but not following the pattern of Jewish festivals, which his congregation did not observe.

And, finally, what of the matters of which Theophilus had been "informed"? The Greek word is "catechise" and it was, and still is, used of the initial instruction which a person is given before baptism or confirmation. It is a technical term: to "catechise" is to instruct, and a "catechism" is the instruction given. And Luke will provide such an instruction, a catechism, in the Lukan Journey (Luke 9.51 – 18.14). It is the great innovation in his Gospel.

Luke's Gospel in Outline

Luke's Birth Narrative is analysed in another chapter. It is certainly very different from Matthew's, although the original idea was his, even if Luke had reservations about some aspects of his story (magi, for example, whom he did not like). So Luke chose the same two starting points as Matthew (the Virgin Birth, and Bethlehem), but otherwise did his own thing. He also chose to insert his Table of Descent later (Luke 3. 23-38), and listed 77 names (11 x 7) instead of the 42 (6 x 7) in Matthew. But his purpose is similar: Jesus is the Son of God and his birth marks the beginning of the final era in the history of the world.

Luke follows Mark less closely than Matthew, but still for the most part re-tells the Markan stories in the Markan order. So, very broadly, in Luke 3 - 9.50 we have Mark 1 - 9.41. The Miraculous Draught of Fishes (Luke 5. 1-11) is his own. The Sermon on the Plain (Luke 6) is his version of Matthew's Sermon on the Mount (Matthew 5 - 7) and the material in Luke 7 is loosely based on Matthew 8 - 9. But at Luke 8.4 he returns to his first source, Mark, with the parable of the Sower and follows him through to Luke 9.50, when he finally heads off on the Lukan Journey. It is not completely straightforward, however, and there are three sections which he leaves out - the so-called Great, and Lesser, Omissions (set out on page 23). Luke's problem is that he has two sources (Matthew as well as Mark), and that the Markan material has already been slightly re-arranged once by Matthew. He also needs both to have his lections fit a rather different calendar than theirs, and to reserve some of their material for future use.

The Journey (Luke 9.51 – 18.14) represents almost a third of Luke's whole Gospel and needs a section to itself, but at Luke 18.15 he re-joins Mark at Mark 10.13 ("They brought babies for him to touch..."). Thereafter he follows Mark to the end, albeit interpreting the Passion of Jesus in a very different way, and ends with a resurrection narrative of his own (Luke 24. 13-53), which is very much in character.

The Lukan Journey

Luke's great innovation, then, is this so-called "Lukan Journey". The journey in question is the journey which Jesus makes from Galilee to Jerusalem at the end of his life and it is called the *Lukan* Journey because only Luke describes it at any length. It is not a long journey in itself (perhaps seventy-five miles), but Luke has a less literal journey in mind - the journey of life. He therefore begins: "As the time approached when he [Jesus] was to be taken up to *heaven*, he set his face *resolutely* towards Jerusalem" (Luke 9.51). The real journey, which every Christian will make, is (in John Bunyan's words[1]) the journey "from this world to that which is to come". Bunyan calls it a "Progress", but as he and Luke knew very well, progress (in the usual sense of the word) is not guaranteed. Many, in their view, will not complete the journey and those that do will need to be resolute and persevering. So Luke has Jesus set off *resolutely* and, in re-telling the parable of the Sower, adds a telling gloss. "The seed in good soil represents those who bring a good and honest heart to the hearing of the word, hold it fast, and *by their perseverance* yield a harvest" (Luke 8.15). A point as important as this needs emphasising. The Christian disciple must be resolute and persevering.

Throughout the journey, then, Luke keeps referring to the need to press on. Jesus is on the move throughout. Nothing is learnt by sitting down. If you want to *learn* (and this section is the *catechism* alluded to in Luke's brief introduction), you have to keep up. So there are many references throughout the journey to Jesus' restless pressing on. Luke 13. 31-33 particularly conveys this sense of urgency. Luke has Jesus reply to the Pharisees: "Go and tell that fox [Herod], 'Listen: today and tomorrow I shall be casting out devils and working cures [there are things to be done]; on the third day I reach my goal [heaven]'. However, I must be on my way *today* and *tomorrow* and the *next day*, because it is unthinkable for a prophet to meet his death anywhere but in Jerusalem." Jesus has to "get there", whatever else he has to do. Discipleship, too, if it is to be serious, must be a "daily" business and Luke glosses Mark 8.34 to this very effect: "If anyone wishes to be a follower of mine, he must leave self behind; *day after day* he must take up his cross, and come with me" (Luke 9.23). "Now and again" is no good.

Above all, in the Lukan Journey, Luke is a free spirit. He is not constrained by the need to follow Mark or Matthew. If he uses their material, as he sometimes does, he uses it freely. And so the Journey, as we would expect, contains most of the stories that are distinctively Lukan - the parables of the Good

Samaritan and the Prodigal Son, for example, and many others. Luke's parables are far less allegorical than Mark's and Matthew's, and therefore much better stories. They are truer to life and contain incidental details that have no allegorical significance, but make them more memorable. They are about ordinary people, rather than kings and fortunes, and they address lots of different subjects (our use of money, penitence, generosity, compassion, and prayer) and are not just warnings ("Look out!"), as Matthew's tend to be. Yet, in spite of this, Luke's intention remains to expound Mark and Matthew, and texts from these sources are still often his starting point.

So, for example, he comes at Luke 10.25 to the lawyer's question, "What must I do to inherit eternal life?" (Mark 12. 28-34; Matthew 22. 34-40). In Mark the lawyer answers the question himself, whereas Matthew has Jesus quote what we now know as the Summary of the Law – to love God with all our heart, and our neighbour as ourselves. And earlier in his Gospel, at Matthew 11. 28-30, he had interpreted these two obligations as the Christian yoke, following Ecclesiasticus 51. 23-30. So Luke thinks how he should illustrate these two duties with a parable or story. In the Jewish way, he takes the last duty first and in the parable of the Good Samaritan shows what it really means to love your neighbour. You show him compassion – as the Samaritan did to the man who was robbed, and as the victorious Israelites had done to their prisoners after defeating Judah in war (Luke 10. 29-37 and 2 Chronicles 28.15). And our duty to God? You "wait on the Lord", seating yourself at his feet, as Mary had done when Jesus arrived at her home, while Martha had worried herself with domestic chores (Luke 10. 38-42). This memorable little story proves Luke's familiarity with Paul's Letters and draws on 1 Corinthians 7. 32-34. The "unmarried or celibate woman [Mary] cares for the Lord's business; her aim is to be dedicated to him in body and spirit; but the married woman [Martha] cares for worldly things...". So both Luke's stories (the Good Samaritan, and Mary and Martha) are prompted by a decision to illustrate a text in Matthew. And, like the faithful midrasher he is, Luke does not "make up" stories out of his head, but finds his inspiration and starting point for them within Scripture, both Jewish and Christian.

In the same way the well-known parable of the Prodigal Son, as it has now come to be called, should really be called the parable of the Two Sons. It is an expansion of Matthew's little parable (Matthew 21. 28-32) and begins with Matthew's very words: "A man had two sons." Matthew's parable is short and to the point. There is no elaboration, no attempt at characterisation, and the message is simple, "You have been warned!". Conversely Luke's parable (Luke 15. 11-32) is memorable and moving, and includes much detail that has no allegorical significance. It is about penitence, a subject close to his heart. Much of the detail Luke draws from the story of Joseph and Jacob (Genesis 37 - 48). Like Joseph, Luke's younger son goes to a distant country, in the grip of famine. He wastes his inheritance, but "comes to his senses" (repents) and decides to return. Like Jacob, his father thinks him dead, and is overwhelmed with emotion to see him again. But the elder brother, who like the Pharisees has done nothing wrong, is, also like them, unable to accept his brother back in a forgiving spirit. Penitence and forgiveness, for Luke, lay at the heart of the Christian life, and had an essential place in any Christian catechism.

Discipleship and the Mind of Christ

We have seen that both Mark and Matthew had an overview of the life of Jesus. For Mark Jesus was the Son of God *incognito*, for Matthew a teacher of wisdom, greater even than Solomon. And Luke, too, had his own perspective. Mark's Messianic Secret made Jesus inscrutable, where Luke wanted his readers (hearers) to *understand* the mind of Christ. Matthew's great discourses for the various festivals in the Jewish calendar also can have had little appeal, or perhaps relevance, since he all but leaves them out. Luke's church may not even have observed Pentecost, and almost certainly did not observe New Year, Tabernacles and Hanukkah.

Luke's essential concern is to portray Jesus as the model Christian and the perfect exemplar of the Christian life. So disciples must, first of all, understand his teaching and, secondly, have some insight into the mind of Jesus so that they can discover the inner disposition that makes the Christian life possible. This teaching is set out, primarily, in the Lukan Journey. Discipleship consists in following. Anyone, therefore, who would learn, must keep up and walk with Jesus on the journey of life. He will then see the Christian life exemplified, and this is Luke's great contribution to Christian thought. The word "disciple" means "someone who *learns* from another", but only Luke emphasises that this learning process takes place through *following*.

Luke's approach is most evident in the modification he makes to the Passion Narrative and this is explained more fully in the chapter on the Passion Narratives. Mark's (and Matthew's) Christ was virtually silent throughout his passion, and dies with a single heart-breaking cry (of despair, even, Luke would have thought) from the cross: "My God, my God, why hast thou forsaken me?" Luke shuddered at the thought and decided to leave this out. He cannot believe that Jesus had said it. Instead he has Jesus talk openly with those who are witnesses of his trial and death. He indicates in what he says to the women of Jerusalem that he feels no self pity (Luke 23. 27-31), in what he says to those who crucified him no bitterness (Luke 23. 32-34), in what he says to the penitent thief a confident hope beyond death (Luke 23. 39-43), and in his last words a sure confidence in commending himself to God (Luke 23. 44-47). These are things that the Christian must learn from the mind of Jesus, as much as from his teaching. But the quality he needs for himself above all else is perseverance.

The Easter Journey

Mark's Gospel ended abruptly and, in Luke's view, inappropriately, with the disciples fleeing the empty tomb in fear. Matthew had put this right by glossing, and added the Great Commission. So what was Luke to do? Above all he wants to explain and, as in the Lukan Journey, all explaining and teaching must be done on the move. So he writes a simple narrative in which Jesus *walks* with two disciples (Cleopas and another) and talks with them *as they journey home* to the village of Emmaus (Luke 24. 13-27). The conversation is artificial

("What do you mean?", Jesus said. "All this about Jesus of Nazareth....", they replied) and what Luke is effectively doing is to provide a reprise. He is going to end his Gospel, and Catechism, with a little revision. He wants to sum up and so has the *conversation* summarise the story of Jesus' ministry, his death, the expectations he aroused, and his resurrection. Jesus needs to be *incognito* to make the conversation possible and Luke wishes him to reveal his identity, as he did to the church in Luke's day, by breaking bread with them and saying the blessing.

The disciples then return to Jerusalem to tell the Eleven (they did not, therefore, belong to the Twelve themselves). And at this point Luke has recourse to a story he has deliberately left out earlier in the Great Omission (Mark 6. 45-52). It is the story in which Jesus walks on the Lake of Galilee and appears to his disciples as they struggle in the midst of a storm. They at first mistake him for a ghost and are terrified, but he says to them, "Take heart! It is I; do not be afraid." At this they are completely dumbfounded; their minds were closed. For Luke this will better serve as a resurrection appearance story, for it has all the same elements. The disciples are terrified and full of unresolved questionings, and Jesus reassures them, as he had done in Mark's story, by telling them, "It is I myself" (Luke 24. 36-43).

This leads on to a final recapitulation (often left out when the story is read in church today). Jesus begins, "This is what I meant by saying that *everything* written about me in *the Law of Moses* and in *the prophets* and *psalms* was bound to be fulfilled" (Luke 24. 44-49). It is important to notice here that it is not just random prophecies that Jesus claims to have fulfilled. It is the *whole* Old Testament – the stories of Abraham and Sarah, of Samuel, of Elijah and Elisha, and of David (in the Book of Psalms as well as elsewhere). His life has provided a complete fulfilment of a whole religious tradition. So he "opens their minds to understand the Scriptures" and represents the message they are to carry (repentance bringing the forgiveness of sins) in a very Lukan way. Jesus then goes with them as far as Bethany, blesses them, and parts from them.

In conclusion we need to remember that Luke is also the author of the Acts of the Apostles, and Jesus' last words in Luke's postscript anticipate its second chapter: "Mark this: I am sending upon you my Father's promised gift" (Luke 24.49). For Jews Pentecost was a commemoration of the Law Giving. For Matthew, a Jewish Christian, the Sermon on the Mount represented a Christian fulfilment, a new Ten Commandments for Christians. But Luke was sufficiently Pauline to know that Christians live, not by the Law, but by the Spirit. So he will provide a different theme for Pentecost (and one that the church was to embrace), whereby the disciples are armed with the Spirit to be his witnesses.

[1] The full title of John Bunyan's book, published in 1678, is *The Pilgrim's Progress: from this world to that which is to come.*

Luke's Gospel in Outline

	Luke	Luke's Source
Luke's purpose in writing his Gospel	1. 1-4	
The Birth Narrative	1.5 - 2	Matthew 1 - 2
John the Baptist, the Table of Descent, and Temptation	3 - 4.13	
The ministry of Jesus begins	4.14 - 6.19	Mark 1.14 - 3.19
The Sermon on the Plain	6. 20-49	Matthew 5 - 7
The ministry of Jesus continues	7	Matthew 8 - 9
The ministry of Jesus continues	8 - 9.50	Mark 4 - 9
The Lukan Journey: A Christian Catechism	9.51 - 18.14	
The ministry of Jesus concludes	18.15 - 21.4	Mark 10.13 - 12
A Passover Discourse	21. 5-end	Mark 13
The Passion Narrative and Empty Tomb	22 - 24.11	Mark 14 - 16.8
An Easter Narrative: A Reprise	24. 12-53	

THE GOSPEL ACCORDING TO JOHN

John's is not a Synoptic Gospel. It cannot be set out in columns as the other three can and it may be helpful, first, to summarise some of the many respects in which it differs from them:

The Synoptic Gospels (Mark, Matthew & Luke)	John's Gospel
Jesus is the Son of God, Messiah, Son of Man (an essentially human figure).	Jesus is the Word of God incarnate (an essentially divine figure).
Jesus announces the coming kingdom of God, part of the drama of the end of the world.	Jesus talks about himself rather than the kingdom of God. There is no expectation of the end of the world.
Jesus teaches in parables.	There are no parables, but rather discourses, mostly in the form of long, one-sided, and sometimes bitter, arguments.
Jesus works miracles in the style of Elijah and Elisha.	There are just seven quite short miracle stories, or signs.
Jesus' ministry is set in Galilee. He comes to Jerusalem only once, at the very end of his life.	Jesus frequently comes to Jerusalem and many of the discourses are set in the temple.
Readers will know about Jesus' family (mother and father, brother and sisters) and about the Twelve (and their names).	Readers will not know that Jesus' mother was called Mary, nor that he had sisters. They will know about the Twelve, but only the names of some of them (they are not listed).
The preparation of an upper room for a Passover Meal, the Institution of the Last Supper, and Judas' betrayal are described in some 20 verses (Mark 14. 12-31).	The Foot-washing, Judas' Betrayal, the Farewell Discourse(s), and the Prayer of Self-dedication occupy five whole chapters, a fifth of John's entire Gospel (John 13 - 17).

Matthew and Luke provide short lections (*pericope*) for a whole year (Mark for roughly six months).	John's Gospel has much longer units (too long to be read as lections in today's church, and not certainly used as lections in the early church).
Mark, Matthew and Luke each have their preferred words and grammatical style, but are written in a generally similar way.	John has a very distinctive, less concise, style with much longer sentences and his own vocabulary.

The Synoptic Gospels belong to a family of Gospels and, on the view taken in this Handbook, are successive re-writes of the same Gospel. What ultimately led to our understanding them better was the opportunity to compare them word for word with each other. By contrast John's Gospel is unique. We cannot get an angle on it. Neither its sources, nor the use of its sources, are clear and very few commentators have found anything interesting or original to say. What passes for commentary is frequently only a paraphrase of the text itself, or an analysis of the meaning of a particular word *within* the Gospel.

The problem is compounded because John's Gospel is also commonly approached reverentially, in a devotional spirit. William Temple's *Readings from St John's Gospel* is one of many commentaries written in this style. It can therefore seem inappropriate, and even churlish, to be critical. You are spoiling something that is precious to other people. The opening verses, read on Christmas Day, are particularly felt to be above criticism and John's Gospel, as a whole, has acquired the status of a sacred text. The risk of disillusion is therefore very great, since many people think it their favourite Gospel. But, as a matter of historical fact, the Synoptic and Johannine Gospels cannot both be right. Their portraits of Jesus are irreconcilable and it must follow that the churches for which John's Gospel was written knew very little about the life of Jesus and perhaps had little interest in it. Indeed Paul himself had never met Jesus and yet became the church's leading advocate. For him the Gospel was a message of salvation.

The Jews

As a beginning it is interesting to note that John's Gospel refers more than sixty times to "the Jews", and that almost all of these references are hostile, many of them bitterly so. They may be Pharisees, Priests, Levites, rulers, officers, crowds, passers-by, or just individuals, but they are all collectively Jews, and Jewish. Their questions are invariably intimidating (John 1.24). They challenge Jesus (John 2.18), are racist (John 4.9), quibble (John 5.10), persecute (John 5.16), murmur disapproval (John 6.41), dispute (John 6. 52), look for a chance to kill him (John 7.1), frighten those who would be disciples (John 7.13; 9.22), hope that he will commit suicide (John 8.22), quarrel among themselves (John 10.19), try to stone him for blasphemy (John 10.31), force him to avoid appearing in public (John 11.54), and all this before the actual Passion gets under way. There is nothing comparable in the Synoptic Gospels.

By contrast, and excluding references to the title, "King of the Jews", there is only one reference to "the Jews" in Matthew (Matthew 28.15), one in Mark (Mark 7.3), and two in Luke (Luke 7.3 and 23.51). This is not to say that everyone is represented sympathetically in the Synoptic Gospels, but it is the *leaders* of the Jews, the Scribes and the Pharisees, whom they hold principally responsible for the death of Jesus. Yet Matthew's Gospel, while written by someone who was himself a Jewish Christian, does ultimately hold the Jews, by their own choice, collectively responsible for the death of Jesus (Matthew 27. 24-26). But this hostility was not apparent during Jesus' ministry.

John's Gospel then, if not obsessed with "the Jews", uses it as a blanket term for a very hostile group. Conversely, the few non-Jewish people portrayed, like the Samaritan woman (John 4. 8-42), and an officer in the royal service (John 4. 46-54), are portrayed sympathetically. Judaea, too, literally the land of the Jews (Jewry), is represented as a hostile place which Jesus avoids (John 4. 43-45, 7.1 and 11. 7-8). By contrast Galilee is welcoming.

The Jews, too, are represented as an alien group whose traditions frequently need explanation. At the wedding in Cana-in-Galilee the six water-jars are described as being "of the kind used for *Jewish* rites of purification" (John 2.6). The cleansing of the temple is prefaced with the explanation, "As it was near the time of the *Jewish* Passover..." (John 3.13; there is a similar reference, too, at John 11.45). Both texts assume a congregation for whom Passover was not a festival. The story of the Feeding of the Five Thousand begins, "It was near the time of Passover, a great *Jewish* festival..." (John 6.4). Chapter 7 begins "As the *Jewish* Feast of Tabernacles was at hand...." (John 7.2). And at the burial of Jesus the Jewish tradition has again to be explained: "They took the body of Jesus and wrapped it, with the spices, in strips of linen cloth *according to Jewish burial customs*" (John 19.40). None of these things would have needed to be explained to Jewish Christians. So, from all of this, we can confidently conclude that John is writing for a non-Jewish and, as we shall see, Pauline church.

The Disciple whom Jesus loved

Another singular feature of John's Gospel is the references in the closing chapters to "the disciple whom Jesus loved", and there has been much inconclusive speculation as to his identity. Some have supposed that it must have been John himself, the author of the Gospel, but since the Gospel was not written until around AD 100, it cannot have been. It is also a very odd phrase in itself, suggesting that this disciple was more loved than the other disciples, Peter even. And why should there be this hint of secrecy? Why is this disciple anonymous, when we would all like to know who he was?

In a recent article in the *Scottish Journal of Theology*[1] Michael Goulder, as so often, has come up with a completely convincing explanation. And the answer is that he is Paul. Not that Paul was *actually* there (at the Last Supper, Crucifixion and so forth), but that the author of John's Gospel *thought* he was – and not without some justification. Yet he was also conscious that he might be challenged, and hence the need for anonymity.

The "disciple whom Jesus loved" makes his first appearance at the Last Supper (John 13. 21-26). Shortly after the disciples have been told by Jesus that he will be betrayed by one of them, Peter wishes to attract Jesus' attention. "The disciple whom he loved was reclining close beside Jesus. So Simon Peter nodded to him and said, 'Ask who it is he means'. That disciple, as he reclined, leaned back close to Jesus and asked, 'Lord, who is it?'". Two things are emphasised – that the disciple was both closest to Jesus and at ease with being so, and that he enjoyed a higher status than Peter, such that Peter had to ask his question through him.

Next, this disciple appears alone of all the disciples with the two Mary's and Jesus' mother at the foot of the cross (John 19. 25-27). "Jesus saw his mother, with the disciple whom he loved standing beside her. He said to her, 'Woman, there is your son'; and to the disciple, 'There is your mother'; and from that moment the disciple took her into his home." Here again, when the other disciples are nowhere to be seen, "the disciple whom Jesus loved" is depicted in a place of honour and, again, completely at ease with his position.

On Easter Sunday morning it is again "the other disciple, the one whom Jesus loved", who accompanies Peter to the empty tomb (John 20. 1-9). On this occasion he outruns Peter and reaches the tomb first. He is the first to peer in, is not the first to enter, but *is* the first to believe: "Then the disciple who had reached the tomb first went in too, and he saw and believed". Again it is odd that he is only identified as he is, and again he is closer to the action than Peter.

Finally, in the postscript to John's Gospel, "the disciple whom Jesus loved" is on the beach with the other disciples, when Jesus appears to them. Again he is first, this time in recognizing Jesus, and tells Peter, "It is the Lord!" (John 21.7). Later he is at hand when Jesus foretells Peter's future. Peter inquires of this other disciple's future as well, but Jesus replies that he has his own plans for him, too. Again it is odd that the anonymity of the disciple whom Jesus loved is preserved, when it would have been so much simpler to name him. There is no suggestion that the evangelist himself does not know who he is. But instead he "is the one who at supper had leaned back close to Jesus to ask the question, 'Lord, who is it that will betray you?'" (John 21.20). Can that have been such a distinguishing thing to do? Why does his name have to be suppressed?

John ends, "It is this same disciple who attests what has here been written. It is in fact *he who wrote it*, and *we* know that his testimony is true" (John 21.24 and again, earlier, at John 19.35). So, to resolve it all, "we" are Pauline Christians; "He who wrote it" is Paul, and where he wrote it is in 1 Corinthians and Galatians. And this Paul, *our* apostle, attests this Gospel, John's. It comes with Paul's seal of approval. But his name is suppressed because the author is wary of asserting something of his hero which he senses others will dispute. But John cannot over-emphasise the point he is making: his account of Jesus' passion and resurrection is absolutely to be trusted and comes from an irrefutable source.

All of this will seem extremely odd and surprising in the first instance, but we need to remember that Paul asserts that he is an apostle in every Letter he writes, and was accepted as such by all the Pauline churches. Moreover, Paul's apostleship owed nothing to any of the disciples but was "by commission from Jesus Christ and from God the Father who raised him from the dead" (Galatians 1.1).

Paul also specifically says: "For the tradition which I handed on to you *came to me from the Lord himself*: that the Lord Jesus, on the night of his arrest, took bread and, after giving thanks to God, broke it and said: 'This is my body, which is for you; do this as a memorial of me.'" (1 Corinthians 11. 23-34). So John is not making anything up. He has it on Paul's own authority that he was there at the Last Supper, and he also had Paul's own word that he owed nothing to the disciples, but received all that he knew "through a revelation of Jesus Christ" (Galatians 1.12). He also believed Paul to have been present at Jesus' death and resurrection. He was no "lying witness" to these events (1 Corinthians. 15. 14-15), but a witness to be trusted.

And the phrase, "the disciple whom Jesus loved"? It may have been suggested by Galatians 2.20. Paul had written: "I have been crucified with Christ: the life I now live is not my life, but the life which Christ lives in me; and my present bodily life is lived by faith in the Son of God, *who loved me* and gave himself for me."

This point is treated in some detail, because it will be new to most people and because it is important in establishing John's sources for what he wrote. But scholars should read Michael Goulder's original article for themselves, a model of biblical scholarship.

Jesus as the Second Adam

We come, finally, to John's overview of the story he told, summarized in two memorable verses: "'God loved the world so much that he gave his only Son, that everyone who has faith in him may not die but have eternal life. It was not to judge the world that God sent his Son into the world, but that through him the world might be saved.'" (John 3. 16-17). This is Jesus himself speaking. It is, of course, John's view, but he attributes it to Jesus.

There is, first of all, nothing remotely comparable in the Synoptic Gospels. Even if we did not know their exact context, we would know immediately that these two verses were from John's Gospel. They are Johannine through and through. The idea of God "sending" his Son into the world, for all that it is Christian orthodoxy today, is not a Synoptic theme. They believed that Jesus was the Son of God, but not in the same sense, not that he was "sent", or "had come down from heaven" (John 6.38). John's verses also speak of salvation and, while the Synoptic Gospels use the metaphor occasionally, theirs are not Gospels of salvation, as John's is. John is not really very interested in the life of Jesus *per se*. He thinks of Jesus as a semi-divine figure, arguably divine without qualification (John 1. 1-14), who knows things before he is told (John 4.39), who does not need to eat and drink (John 4. 31-34) and who had foreknowledge of his own future (John 18.4). The story of the Samaritan woman at Jacob's Well ends with descriptions of characteristic Samaritan enthusiasm for Jesus. They press him to stay with them and say of Jesus: "We know that this is in truth the Saviour of the world" (John 4.42). That is the testimony of John and of the Pauline churches.

It is not surprising, therefore, that John's Gospel begins, famously, with the Creation of the world. Jesus is the Word of God, and his agent in creation (John 1. 1-14). "All that came to be was alive with his life" (there was no other). And there is the subsequent irony that, although the world "owed its being to him" (John 1.10), it did not recognize him. Whatever we make of this, John's is a very deliberate beginning. Luke had traced Jesus' genealogy back to Adam, and finally God (Luke 3.38), but this is different again. Luke's genealogy was slotted in after the story of John the Baptist's ministry, but this is hugely more powerful. John may immediately move on to the ministry of John the Baptist, but his introduction is cosmic. He was not attracted to the Synoptic Birth Narratives, which tell a very human story.

John begins his Gospel with the Creation because he plans to portray the story of Jesus, "the Word of God made flesh", who redeems the world, as an act of Re-creation. As a Pauline Christian he will very probably have known most of Paul's Letters and in both Romans 5. 12-21, and 1 Corinthians 15. 45-49, Paul had represented Jesus as the Second Adam. The First Adam, the Adam of the Creation Story in Genesis 2.5 - 3.24, was the cause of Man's downfall. The Second Adam, Jesus, is the occasion of Man's salvation. "By the wrongdoing of that one man [Adam] death established its reign", but now, through an infinitely "greater measure of God's grace", shall those who receive God's gift of righteousness "live and reign through the one man, Jesus Christ" (Romans 5.17). "The first man [Adam] was made 'of the dust of the earth': the second man [Jesus] is from heaven....As we have worn the likeness of the man made of dust, so we shall wear the likeness of the heavenly man" (1 Corinthians 15. 45-49). This will be John's theme, explicit in places, but implicit in his whole Gospel.

There had been a Creation at the very beginning of the world, and John's Gospel will tell the story of Jesus as an act of Re-creation. Neither Paul, nor John, seem to have known or, if they did know, seem to have cared very much about the circumstances of the earthly life of Jesus. If we had only Paul's Letters and John's Gospel, it is surprising how little we would know. Most of John's Gospel comprises discourses. Jesus may be talking to his disciples (chapters 10, and 14-16), or with individuals like Nicodemus and the Samaritan Woman (chapters 3-4), or with "the Jews" (chapters 7-9). These are not all discourses in the strict sense - those with Nicodemus and the Samaritan woman are more like conversations, and those with "the Jews" more like arguments. But the interventions, whether friendly or hostile, are always brief. Jesus is in total command and the interruptions serve only to carry the conversation forward and give Jesus the opportunity to make his points. In short, the conversations, with disciples, individuals, or enemies, are always very one-sided.

The Passion Narratives in all four Gospels are analysed and compared in a later chapter, and to avoid unnecessary repetition a full account of John's Passion Narrative is deferred until then. But it may be helpful now to give just three examples of the way in which John drew upon the two Creation Stories in Genesis 1-3 in telling the story of the trial and crucifixion of Jesus.

It is significant, in the first place, that John chooses "a garden" as the setting for the arrest of Jesus (John 18.1). We always tend to conflate the Gospels and, since Mark (and Matthew) set the temptation of Jesus in "Gethsemane", refer to "the *garden* of Gethsemane". But there is nothing in the text to suggest that Gethsemane was a garden. The garden that John has in mind is the Garden of *Eden*, the scene of Adam's temptation and downfall. So a garden, too, will be the scene of Jesus' temptation and triumph.

Again, when Pilate presents Jesus to the crowd, he does so with the words, "Behold the Man" (John 19.6). This can seem a quite innocent remark, but for Pauline Christians Jesus is indeed "the Man" with a capital M, the Second Adam, who will restore our fortunes and bring us salvation. In short, Pilate speaks truer than he knows.

Then, finally, at the moment of his death, John has Jesus say, "It is accomplished" (John 19.30). This *could* be taken to mean, "That is the end", but again it is not what John intended. He means "the *salvation of mankind* has been accomplished". For God created the world in six days and "finished" his work of creation as the Sabbath was about to begin (Genesis 2. 1-2). And so now, on the sixth day (a Friday), Jesus also finishes, completes, "accomplishes" *his* work of *re*-creation, to enjoy a

Sabbath rest himself, appearing to his disciples on Easter Day and then again a week later.

Further detail will be added in the chapter on the Passion Narratives. But, for all that there is still much to puzzle over, John's Gospel is now emerging as a Gospel for Pauline Christians, based on Paul's testimony, and interpreting the life of Jesus as he interpreted it.

[1] For Paul as "the disciple whom Jesus loved", see "An Old Friend Incognito" by Michael Goulder in the *Scottish Journal of Theology*, volume 45, pages 487-513. The article is stunning in its originality and brilliance.

John's Gospel in Outline

1. 1-14	Jesus is God's Word come into the world	
1. 15-51	The Testimony of John	Bethany beyond Jordan
2. 1-11	Jesus turns water into wine (the first sign)	Cana in Galilee
2. 12-25	Jesus cleanses the Temple	In the temple at Jerusalem
3. 1-21	Nicodemus	Jerusalem
3. 22-36	John and his disciples baptize	Aenon, near Salim, in Judaea
4. 1-42	The Samaritan Woman	Sychar in Samaria
4. 43-54	Jesus heals the officer's son (the second sign)	Cana in Galilee
5	Jesus heals a crippled man (the third sign)	The Sheep Pool at Bethesda (Jerusalem)
6. 1-15	The feeding of the five thousand (the fourth sign)	The far shore of the Sea of Galilee
6. 16-21	Jesus walks on the sea (the fifth sign)	On the Sea of Galilee
6. 22-71	A fierce dispute: "I am the bread of life"	The synagogue in Capernaum
7. 1-9	In conversation with his brothers	Galilee
7. 10-36	Jesus disputes with the Jews	In the temple in Jerusalem
7. 37-52	A further dispute	In the temple in Jerusalem
8. 1-12	The woman taken in adultery	In the temple in Jerusalem
8. 12-59	A further dispute: "I am the light of the world"	In the temple in Jerusalem

9	Jesus heals a blind man (the sixth sign)	In the temple in Jerusalem
10	A parable: "I am the good shepherd"	In the temple in Jerusalem
10. 21-39	Jesus disputes during the festival of Hanukkah	In the temple in Jerusalem
10.40 - 11.44	The raising of Lazarus (the seventh sign): "I am the resurrection and I am life"	Across the Jordan
12. 1-11	Mary anoints Jesus	In Lazarus' home in Bethany
12. 12-50	Going up to the Festival	On his way to Jerusalem
13. 1-30	The Foot-washing; Judas is identified as the traitor	During supper
13.31 - 16.33	The Farewell Discourse	During supper
17	Jesus' Prayer	After these words
18 - 19	The Passion Narrative	In and around Jerusalem
20. 1-18	The empty tomb - Jesus appears to Mary	At the tomb
20. 19-23	Jesus appears to the disciples	Behind locked doors
20. 24-31	Jesus appears to Thomas and the disciples	In the same room
21	Jesus appears on the beach to his disciples	By the Sea of Galilee (Tiberias)

THE BIRTH NARRATIVES

Today the Birth Narratives are almost always associated with Christmas and it is rare for them to be read or discussed at any other time. Christmas, however, was not a festival of the early church and almost certainly only dates from the fourth century. The first reference to it occurs in the Philocalian Calendar, which dates from 354 and represents the practice of the Roman church in 336. The entry reads "25 Dec: natus Christus in Betleem Judeae". There is little doubt that it was chosen, perhaps at the Council of Nicaea in 325, to replace the old Roman festival of Natalis Solis Invicti (the Birth of the Unconquered Sun), the winter solstice.

The Council, over which the Emperor Constantine himself presided, discussed many practical issues but is chiefly remembered today for its Creed, which sought to define the church's belief in Jesus as the God-Man. It is very probable, therefore, that Christmas originally celebrated, not the *birth* of Jesus (a historical event), but the *Incarnation* (the new Nicaean doctrine of how Jesus was, at the same time, both human and divine). It would be for this reason that the Gospel for the day has always been John 1. 1-14 ("The Word became flesh and dwelt among us"), rather than a reading from one of the Birth Narratives. Constantine also decided at about this time that the first Church of the Holy Nativity in Bethlehem should be built and Sunday became a public holiday.

Disentangling the Two Stories

The Christmas story is best known to most people today from Nativity Plays, Carol Services, Christmas cribs, and hymns. All of these conflate Matthew's and Luke's quite different stories into a single text. A scene, a reading, is taken from one Gospel, and the next scene, the next reading, from the other. As a result the two stories have become hopelessly muddled in most people's minds and, if we are to understand what Matthew and Luke intended, we have first to disentangle them.

Matthew begins with the Table of Descent (Matthew 1. 1-17), which is explained in the chapter on the Gospel according to

Matthew. He then goes on to describe how Mary gives birth to Jesus without sexual intercourse (Matthew 1. 18-25). The story takes a new turn when magi (astrologers) from the east alarm King Herod with their news of a child who has been "born to be King of the Jews" (Matthew 2. 1-6). They seek his advice on where they might find this child and Herod directs them to Bethlehem on the basis of the prophecy in Micah 5 (Matthew 2. 7-8). So the magi set out and, when they find the child, present their gifts of gold, frankincense and myrrh (Matthew 2. 9-12). But, on reflection, they decide not to alert Herod to their discovery, as he had asked them to do, and so allow Joseph, Mary, and Jesus to escape to Egypt (Matthew 2. 13-15). Herod, meanwhile, takes his revenge on the children of Bethlehem with the Massacre of the Innocents (Matthew 2. 16-18). Finally, when Joseph learns in a dream of Herod's death, he take his family back to the land of Israel and settles in Nazareth (Matthew 2. 19-23).

Luke's story is quite different. He follows Matthew in respect of the Virgin Birth, and in having Jesus born in Bethlehem, but he leaves out all the material in Matthew 2. So there is nothing in Luke's Gospel about Herod, or the magi, or the star, or the Flight into Egypt, or the Massacre of the Innocents. Instead Luke adds an annunciation, or rather *two* annunciations, telling the story of the annunciation, birth and circumcision of John the Baptist and Jesus in parallel. Luke knew that John had been Jesus' forerunner in respect of his ministry, and he therefore now also makes him Jesus' forerunner in respect of his birth. So he begins by telling the story of Gabriel's annunciation of John's birth to his father, Zechariah (Luke 1. 5-25), and follows this with a similar annunciation of Jesus' birth to Mary (Luke 1. 26-38). John's birth and circumcision (Luke 1. 57-80) is then followed by Jesus' birth (Luke 2. 1-7) and circumcision (Luke 2. 21-40). And having decided to leave out Matthew's magi, Luke instead introduces the shepherds, who acclaim his birth in their place (Luke 2. 8-20). Next, Jesus is circumcised in the temple at Jerusalem (Luke 2. 21-24), where Simeon and Anna recognise him as the Lord's Messiah (Luke 2. 25-40). Finally, at the age of twelve, Jesus is taken by his parents to Jerusalem, where he impresses the teachers with his wisdom (Luke 2. 41-52).

Matthew's Sources

What, then, were Matthew's and Luke's sources for the stories they told? Mark's Gospel was their principal source for the ministry and death of Jesus, but they had no similar source for his birth. So they looked to Scripture for enlightenment. If Jesus was the Son of God and Messiah, his birth will have been foretold and foreshadowed there.

Most people today will think immediately of Micah 5.2 and Isaiah 7. 10-17, because they are often read in carol services, and because both prophecies are actually quoted in Matthew's text. First of all, centuries beforehand, Micah had predicted that the Messiah would be born in Bethlehem and, clearly, here was a prophecy awaiting fulfilment. The second prophecy was less obvious. Isaiah predicts the birth of a child, to be called Immanuel, as a sign that a threat of war has passed. But it is set in a very specific historical context, which has no relevance. However, Immanuel means "God is with us", and what had the birth of Jesus been but a fulfilment of that. Matthew also noticed that the Greek text of the Old Testament (the Septuagint, or LXX for short) had translated the Hebrew word for "young woman", the child's mother, as "virgin". Here again Matthew saw God's hand at work and thought of the mistranslation as providential. If Jesus is the Immanuel, then perhaps his, too, was a virgin birth.

This was a beginning, but it did not take Matthew all the way. But both he and Luke thought of Jesus as fulfilling, not just individual prophecies, but the Old Testament as a whole. And Matthew's church will probably have begun reading his Gospel on the fifth Sabbath of the Jewish year (just after Passover), when their Old Testament readings would be successive blocks of Genesis (about three or four chapters a week). Matthew therefore bases his Birth Narrative on the stories of Jacob, Esau and Joseph, which his Jewish Christian congregation will have heard read as their first lesson.

Joseph, by coincidence, was also Jesus' father's actual name and so Matthew models him on Joseph of old. Like Joseph of old, Matthew's Joseph is a dreamer of dreams - at every juncture in the story Joseph is warned *in a dream* of impending events. So an angel of the Lord appears to him in a dream explaining why he should not set the marriage contract aside when he discovers that Mary is pregnant (Matthew 1.20). The angel appears in a dream again to warn him to flee to Egypt (Matthew 2.13), and on a third occasion to tell him about Herod's death (Matthew 2.19).

But the story of two brothers, Jacob and Esau, was also suggestive. Each also had another name. Jacob's other name was Israel, and Esau's was Edom. Esau was the older brother, but Genesis 27 describes how Jacob supplants his older brother by securing his father's blessing in his place. Isaac says to him, prophetically, "Peoples shall serve you, nations *bow down* to you" (Genesis 27.29). And this story provides Matthew with the basis for his story of the rivalry between another Edom (Herod) and another Israel (Jesus). For Herod was the King of Edom, while Jesus was the founder of the new Israel, the church. Matthew's story will therefore describe how Jesus supplants Herod as "King of the Jews", a title to which they both lay claim, as Jacob had supplanted Esau. Details are added from other sources. Herod is also another Pharaoh (they are both ruthless tyrants) and Pharaoh's slaughter of all newborn Jewish boys, on hearing of the birth of Moses (Exodus 1. 15-22), is Matthew's source for Herod's slaughter of the innocents.

Our interest today is more narrowly focused on the star, the Magi, and their gifts, since these all feature in Christmas Nativity Plays (the Slaughter of the Innocents does not!). And again we shall find their source in Scripture. For Joseph of old had also dreamt that the sun and moon and eleven stars bowed down before him (Genesis 37. 5-11) and, further, had become an interpreter of other people's dreams as a prisoner in Egypt, so much so that he supplanted the wise men of Egypt. So when his brothers later visit Egypt in time of famine, they bring him gifts (Genesis 43. 11-12). In the same way Matthew describes how Magi from the east came to *bow down* before another Joseph's child, Jesus, and bring him the gifts of Scripture - gold (Psalm 72. 10-11, 15), frankincense, and myrrh (both many times mentioned in the Song of Songs as, for example, at 3.6). The text from Psalm 72 also explains why the Magi are sometimes, wrongly, confused with kings. But what of the star? Each Christmas there are articles trying to identify it with known meteors and the like. But Matthew's star was almost certainly a *theological* star: "A star shall come forth out of Jacob, a comet arise from Israel" (Numbers 24.17).

Luke's Sources

While the Isaiah and Micah prophecies in Matthew will have appealed to Luke, the story of Herod and the magi did not. So he left them out. Perhaps it was his dislike of magi because, as we know from Acts (Acts 13. 6-12) he had no time for magic (Elymas, the sorcerer, is described as a magus, or sorcerer, and is rebuked and blinded by Paul for opposing the Gospel). But his church, like Matthew's, was also reading Genesis, and Luke therefore thought to base his Birth Narrative on a different story - the birth of Isaac to Abraham and Sarah (Genesis 17. 15-22 and 21. 1-2). Their counterparts in Luke's story are Zechariah and Elizabeth. So, just as Abraham laughed and was disbelieving when told that his elderly wife, Sarah, would have a child, Luke has Zechariah, another sceptic, disbelieve Gabriel, when first told that *his* elderly wife, Elizabeth, would give birth to *their* first child, John the Baptist.

For the birth of Jesus to Mary, Luke goes to the story of the birth of Samuel to Hannah (1 Samuel 1). Many people have remarked how very similar Hannah's Song (1 Samuel 2) is to Mary's Song, Magnificat (Luke 1. 46-55). Canticles, as we now call them, are indeed a feature of Luke's story and Zechariah's Song celebrating the birth of John the Baptist (Luke 1. 68-79) is very similar to David's, when he had defeated Saul to become the undisputed king of Israel (2 Samuel 22). And for the Song of Simeon (Luke 2. 29-32) Luke found inspiration, not in an Old Testament canticle, but in a prophecy of Isaiah (Isaiah 40. 1-5).

But Luke's omission of the story of Herod and the magi left him with the need for further material. How should he tell the story of Jesus' birth in Bethlehem? He first introduces the census, for which no historical evidence can be found, to explain how Jesus, whose home was in Nazareth, came to be born in Bethlehem. Then the Matthaean saying at Matthew 8.20

("Foxes have their holes, the birds their roosts; but the Son of Man has *nowhere to lay his head*") may have suggested that Jesus was born in a stable. And finally, like Matthew, he needed someone to acclaim the birth of Jesus and he replaces Matthew's magi with shepherds. The message of the angels ("Glory to God in highest heaven, and on earth his peace for men on whom his favour rests") conflates two texts from Isaiah (Isaiah 6.3 and 9. 6-7).

Samuel was a precocious child and, as he grew up, none of his words went unfulfilled. His word had authority throughout Israel. So, too, was Jesus precocious. When he was twelve he amazed those who talked with him in the temple (Luke 2. 41-52), as Samuel had done in Shiloh (1 Samuel 2.18 and 3. 19-21).

Conclusion

Many people have always felt that the Birth Narratives were more story than history and our study supports this view. Matthew and Luke both believed that Jesus was the Messiah and the fulfilment of all Old Testaments hopes and expectations. They felt that his birth, like those of Isaac, Samuel, and Samson, must have been auspicious and so they each created their stories, not by inventing them or thinking them up, but through a careful study of Scripture. They believed that Jesus must have been born of a virgin, not because they had any historical information to that effect, but because Scripture led them to think that he must have been. Others, of course, have misunderstood their stories and built upon them doctrines which Matthew and Luke themselves would never have endorsed. But it was not inevitable that this should happen and we shall appreciate their stories ourselves all the more when we understand how they were constructed.

Note: Those wishing to explore the subject in more detail will find it explained at greater length in Michael Goulder's *Midrash and Lection in Matthew* (SPCK 1974) and *Luke, a New Paradigm* (Sheffield Academic Press 1989).

THE PASSION NARRATIVES

Each of the Gospels has already been analysed in turn, but it is worth returning to the Passion Narratives, even if it involves a degree of repetition, because they are so central to everything.

As we have seen, Mark's is the original Gospel. He believed Jesus to have died on 14th Nisan (that is, on the first day of the Feast of Passover). It was a Friday and Pontius Pilate was Procurator of Judaea (he was Procurator from AD 26-36). In theory this yields two possible dates for the death of Jesus, but Mark may have got it wrong. It is, in principle, unlikely that executions would take place during Passover. It was a time of great religious significance and the Jewish Council would have had other things to do. What Mark may have confused was the actual date of Jesus' death, and the date of its annual commemoration. For Mark's Passion Narrative, alone of the four, has clues that it was used each year as part of a twenty-four-hour vigil. This commemoration will have begun on the afternoon of 13th Nisan, and involved moving every three hours to the scene of each next incident in the story. But it would have ceased in AD 70, when Jerusalem was destroyed, and the sites were no longer accessible.

The Early Pattern of Commemoration: A 24-hour Vigil

Mark prefaces his Passion Narrative with a Passover Discourse (Mark 13). Its purpose is to alert the church to the possibility that this Passover might be the Passover when Jesus will return in glory and judgement. The discourse ends: "Keep awake, then, for you do not know when the master of the house is coming. *Evening* or *midnight, cock-crow* or *early dawn* - if he comes suddenly, he must not find you asleep" (Mark 13. 35-36). The early church, then, should not go to bed on the night of Passover. They must keep a vigil.

Mark's Passion Narrative begins when Passover is still two days off (Mark 14.1), but the story proper begins at Mark 14.12: "Now on the first day of Unleavened Bread...." (that is, on the

71

first day of Passover, 14th Nisan). The following sequence of events can then be deduced:

3.00pm (on 13th Nisan): The Anointing at Bethany

6.00pm (at dusk, and therefore now 14th Nisan): The Last Supper begins (*"In the evening* Jesus came to the house....")

9.00pm: The vigil in Gethsemane (Jesus goes away and returns *three times*, saying "Were you not able to stay awake for *one hour?"*)

12 midnight: Jesus is arrested and his trial before the Jewish Council begins

3.00am (Cock-crow): Peter's Denial ("Then *the cock crew a second time*; and Peter remembered....")

6.00am: The Interrogation of Jesus by Pilate begins (*"When morning came*...they led him away and handed him over to Pilate.")

9.00am: The Crucifixion ("The hour of the crucifixion was *nine in the morning*....")

12 noon: Darkness falls (*"At midday* a darkness fell over the whole land....")

3.00pm: Jesus dies ("And *at three* Jesus cried aloud....")

6.00pm (the day's end): The Deposition ("By this time *evening had come*....")

These indications of time, to be found within Mark's text, are compelling evidence for its use as a vigil. Equally, their absence in the other Gospels indicates that the practice had probably lapsed.

"Let the Scriptures be Fulfilled" (Mark's story)

Mark believed that Jesus was the Messiah, or Son of God, and that his whole life was anticipated and foretold in the Old Testament. He was not alone in this, but it gives his Passion Narrative a distinctive emphasis. In his view the story of Jesus was predestined, predetermined, and scripted like a play. Jesus' life had to be how it was going to be and, to ensure this, his identity had been concealed. This, the Messianic Secret, is explained in the chapter on the Gospel according to Mark, but it gives the Passion Narrative a particular poignancy. We hope against hope that Jesus' death may somehow be averted, but by remaining silent he does nothing to help his cause. As he tells the disciples at the Last Supper, "The Son of Man is going the way *appointed for him in the Scriptures*" (Mark 14.21). So it is no good hoping. It is a phrase he repeats again at his arrest: "Do you take me for a bandit, that you have come out with swords and cudgels to arrest me? But *let the Scriptures be fulfilled...*" (Mark 14. 48-49).

Thereafter Jesus lapses into almost total silence. He is an enigmatic figure in a world of his own. When he is asked by the High Priest at his trial, "Have you no answer to the charges that these witnesses bring against you?" Mark concludes: "But he kept silence; he made no reply" (Mark 14.60). Again, before Pilate, he is asked, "Have you nothing to say in your defence? You see how many charges they are bringing against you." But the outcome is the same. "To Pilate's astonishment, Jesus made no further reply" (Mark 15.5). He is silent before the crowd and silent at his crucifixion. Only at the moment of death is his silence broken with the harrowing words from Psalm 22: "My God, my God, why hast thou forsaken me?" (Psalm 22.1).

So what are these Scriptures that must find fulfilment in Jesus' death? They are the Old Testament, obviously, and Mark has very many more texts in mind than the casual reader will realise. But the Psalms as a whole, and Psalm 22 in particular, were a rich source of material.

The effect of these fulfilments is to make Mark's much the bleakest of the Passion Narratives. The reader is full of foreboding from the beginning, and progressively Jesus is stripped of everything - his disciples (who run away), his dignity, his clothes, his God even, and his life. It gets worse and worse as the story progresses. At various points there can seem to be some possibility of reprieve, but our hopes are always dashed. And Jesus himself, having made the good confession at his trial, says nothing further, and refuses to answer questions. His final cry of dereliction is entirely in character. Mark portrays Jesus as feeling totally abandoned.

But in many ways Mark's is also much the most moving account of Jesus' death. The story has a tremendous momentum and a surprising number of people are drawn in, most of them against their will (Judas, Barabbas, Pilate, and

Simon of Cyrene). We feel for them as they struggle with their various roles, dealt out to them like parts in a play. We do not so much blame them for what they do, as tremble that we ourselves might so easily have been assigned their roles.

Matthew's Story

Matthew was the first to re-write Mark's Gospel and he almost doubles its length. But he is not really interested in developing the Passion Narrative. In large measure he just copies out, often word for word, what Mark has written. Mark's emphasis is lost, but nothing significant is left out. And what Matthew adds he finds, like Mark, in Scripture. There is no evidence of his having any independent historical source.

In particular Matthew's is a more anti-Jewish Gospel than Mark's. As explained in the chapter on the Gospel according to Matthew, there is reason to suppose that he thought of himself as a Christian Scribe and he is a particularly bitter critic of the Jewish Scribes and Pharisees (Matthew 23). It is therefore in character that he makes the Jews personally, and for all time, responsible for the death of Jesus. Only Matthew has them say, when Jesus is condemned to death, "His blood be on us and on our children" (Matthew 27.25).

In the same way he elaborates the story of Judas, specifying the sum as thirty silver pieces (following Zechariah 11.12), and describes how Judas returned the money and hanged himself. In Matthew's mind this was an appropriately Scriptural death, for had not Ahitophel, who conspired against David, also gone away and hanged himself? (2 Samuel 17.23).

For the rest Matthew follows Mark faithfully. He adds a few small glosses, introduces two earthquakes (Matthew 27. 50-54 and 28. 1-2), and adds the setting of the guard. He found Scriptural precedent for these as well, but they are just additions to the story and do not involve any radical re-interpretation .

Understanding the Mind of Christ (Luke's Story)

Luke, by contrast with Matthew, went for a major re-write and has made discipleship his principal theme. For Luke, a Christian is a person who follows in Jesus' footsteps, and who learns from him as he does so. Jesus, then, represents the Christian ideal. He is a model Christian and, if any disciple is to follow Jesus, he must not only learn what Jesus teaches, but must also try to understand the mind of Jesus, and what made him the person he was. And Luke, of course, is at hand to help. That is the role of a Christian evangelist.

So Luke's first aim in re-writing the Passion Narrative is to enable his Christian congregation to understand what Jesus felt about his death. Mark's Passion Narrative is no help at all. His Jesus is completely inscrutable. He only has Jesus say, "My God, my God, why hast thou forsaken me?", which suggests despair. But could Jesus really have lost faith like that? Luke thought, "absolutely not". So he leaves it out and has Jesus say four quite different things instead: (to the crowd) "Daughters of Jerusalem, do not weep for me...." (Luke 23. 27-31); (with the soldiers in mind) "Father, forgive them; they do not know what they are doing" (Luke 23.34); (to the penitent thief) "I tell you this: today you shall be with me in Paradise" (Luke 23.43); and finally (at the moment of death) "Father, into thy hands I commit my spirit" (Luke 23.46). These four sayings deserve detailed analysis, since they transform the story that Luke has inherited.

As, then, Jesus is led away to his death he says to the crowd: "Daughters of Jerusalem, do not weep for me; no, weep for yourselves and your children. For the days are coming..." (Luke 23. 27-31). Hard times lie ahead. Present day observance of Good Friday does not reckon this as one of the "seven sayings from the cross" (hopelessly misconceived, anyway, since the Gospels cannot be conflated without missing their whole point) and it is therefore generally overlooked. But Luke (and only Luke) wants us to understand that Jesus felt no self-pity. He did not feel sorry for himself. It was not his tragedy, but theirs. And so this insight should inform the life of his disciples as well.

So Jesus is crucified and asks forgiveness for his executors: "Father, forgive them; they do not know what they are doing" (Luke 23.34). Forgiveness is a characteristically Lukan theme, as, for example, in the parables of the Lost Sheep, the Lost Coin, and the Lost, or Prodigal, Son (Luke 15). But Jesus not only teaches forgiveness - he practises it. He feels no bitterness at what the soldiers are doing to him and, again, exemplifies the life he taught. And the idea, or inspiration, for this may have come from the stoning of Stephen (Acts 7. 54-60). For Stephen had also said, as he died, "Lord, do not hold this sin against them."

Next Jesus says to one of the criminals executed with him, "I tell you this: today you shall be with me in Paradise" (Luke 23.43). So Jesus is not despondent, but full of hope for the future.

His final words are: "Father, into thy hands I commit my spirit" (Luke 23.46). It is difficult to conceive of a sentiment more different than Mark and Matthew had conveyed with their, "My God, my God, why hast thou forsaken me?" (Mark 15.34). Luke lifts the gloom and portrays Jesus as trusting, loving, and forgiving to the end. His faith, as Stephen's had been, is undiminished, for Stephen, too, had said, "Lord Jesus, receive my spirit", at the moment of death (Acts 7.59).

Luke's second major innovation is to re-arrange the trials of Jesus. Mark and Matthew have two trials - before the Jewish Council (from midnight to 3.00am) and before Pilate (from 6.00am to just before 9.00am). Luke describes four trials and they all take place between 6.00am (daybreak) and 9.00am. The first trial is before the Jewish Council (Luke 22. 66-71), the second before Pilate (Luke 23. 1-5), the third before Herod (Luke 23. 6-12), and the fourth before Pilate, again (Luke 23. 13-25). One possibility, here, is that Luke has aligned the trials of Jesus with Paul's four trials, before the Jewish Council (Acts 23. 1-10), before Felix (Acts 24. 1-23), before Festus (Acts 25. 6-12), and before King Agrippa (Acts 25.23 – 26.32). Jesus lives on in his disciples so that the trials which they endure are his trials also.

However, the outcome of these four trials is to prove Jesus' *innocence*. This is another Lukan emphasis (Luke 23.4, 23. 13-16, and 23.22). Even the centurion, an impartial representative of the Roman world, who had "seen it all", concludes, "Beyond all doubt this man was *innocent*" (Luke 23.47). This fits better with Luke's theme than Mark's, "Truly this man was a Son of God" (Mark 15.39).

And, finally, Luke shows a greater understanding of the frailty of the disciples than Mark and Matthew do. On the Mount of Olives (Luke does not mention Gethsemane) the disciples only fall asleep because they are "worn out by grief" (Luke 22.45). It is not that they do not care. Similarly Peter gets within sight of Jesus in the High Priest's house and, after his vehement denials, Luke says that "the Lord turned and looked at Peter" (Luke 22.61). There are not the tears and heartbreak so characteristic of Mark. This is a moment of shame, but also perhaps of reassurance.

It is difficult to do justice to Luke's achievement in just a few paragraphs, but he has transformed the story which he found in Mark and Matthew. Where Mark's story, in particular, moves us to tears, Luke's is inspirational.

Luke defers the story of Judas' death for later use in the Acts of the Apostles, when his successor is chosen by lot (Acts 1. 15-22). But he thought hanging too easy a death for someone who had betrayed for money and instead has Judas "fall forward on the ground, and burst open, so that his entrails poured out". This is very reminiscent of the death of Jezebel, who had organised Naboth's death so that Ahab could acquire his vineyard, and (as Elijah had prophesied) was thrown from her bedroom window to a horrible death below (2 Kings 9. 30-37).

A Second Adam (John's Story)

John's Gospel stands apart from the other three and its provenance has always been less clear. We also reach the beginning of the Passion Narrative much sooner than in the other Gospels. It begins at chapter 13 with a sort of Last Supper (the Foot-washing, Judas' Betrayal, but no Supper as such) and then proceeds with the long Farewell Discourse.

It is also at the Last Supper that "the disciple whom Jesus loved" makes his first appearance. His identification as Paul is crucial to our understanding of John's Gospel and is explained in the chapter on the Gospel according to John. For John's is a Gospel for Pauline Christians and its Passion Narrative is built around the Pauline idea of Jesus as the Second Adam (Romans 5. 12-21; 1 Corinthians 15. 20-28, 45-49). The First Adam was the cause of man's downfall at the creation of the world; the Second

Adam (Jesus) is the cause of our redemption and the author of a New Creation.

Whereas the Synoptic Gospels (Mark, Matthew and Luke) have Jesus die on 14th Nisan, John dates it a day earlier on 13th Nisan: "It was *before* the Passover Festival..." (John 13.1). He may have known better than they did, or he too may have had a theological rationale. For if Jesus is "the Lamb of God" (a Johannine title not found in the Synoptic Gospels), then it would be fitting if he should die on the *eve* of Passover, when the Paschal lambs were being killed.

For simplicity we pick up John's story at chapter 18. People today commonly refer to the "Garden" of Gethsemane, but this is a misreading. Mark and Matthew have Gethsemane; Luke has the Mount of Olives, and John simply, "a garden". But, as already explained in the chapter on John's Gospel, the garden that he has in mind is not Gethsemane, but the Garden of *Eden*. That was the scene of Adam's surrender to temptation, and will be the setting for Jesus' triumph over temptation.

He is interrogated by the High Priest (not the Jewish Council), is rudely treated, but not specifically condemned. This section (John 18. 12-27) is really more concerned with the story of Peter's Denial. The real trial, if one can call it that, will be before Pilate (John 18.28 - 19.16), and this is described at very much greater length than in the other Gospels. Here the dialogue is reminiscent of the earlier discourses and arguments. Pilate tries to mediate between Jesus and "the Jews", but when he talks with Jesus there is no real communication. There is a poignant moment, already recalled in an earlier chapter, when Pilate presents Jesus to the crowd and says, "Behold the Man" (John 19.5). It is an odd thing to say and could be taken to mean, "Here he is". But John wishes his readers to understand it theologically. He means, "Here is the Man (with a capital M), the Second Adam". And, as in Matthew's Gospel, John makes clear that the responsibility for Jesus' death rests with "the Jews".

This brings us to the crucifixion itself, and here John first adds the story of the tunic, which cannot be divided and for which the soldiers therefore cast lots (John 19. 23-24). It again recalls the story of Adam and Eve, where the same word, "tunic", is used. But where they clothed themselves with tunics to hide their guilt, Jesus is divested of his tunic to accomplish his work of redemption.

Jesus commends his mother to "the disciple whom Jesus loved", drinks from a sponge soaked in sour wine and says, "It is accomplished" (John 19. 28-30). This carries echoes of the first Creation Story (Genesis 1.1 - 2.3). For in Genesis 1 great play is made of the fact that God "finished" his work of creation on the sixth day, and so rested. In the same way Jesus has now "finished" his work of recreation and so can look forward to a Sabbath of resurrection appearances. *His* work is done as well.

Finally we come to a last puzzling addition. Because Jesus has already died, his legs are not broken, as are the legs of the two other prisoners, but instead a spear is thrust into his side from which blood and water flow. This, too, has theological significance, for just as Eve was taken from Adam's side, so now blood and water (representing the church's sacraments of Baptism and the Lord's Supper) flow from Jesus' side. In his First Letter John had written, "There are three witnesses, the Spirit, the water and the blood" (1 John 5.6). The Spirit is the Spirit of Jesus, which he now hands over. As John says, "He bowed his head and gave up [handed over] his spirit" (John 19.30). But this analysis still leaves many things unexplained. John's Gospel is rarely transparent and the real significance of many details in his story still escape us.

In Conclusion

In analysing the Birth Narratives we have already seen how consolidating two separate stories (Matthew's and Luke's) into one, results in a lack of definition and focus. And this is even more the case when *four* Passion Narratives are condensed, with extracts from each story interspersed. There may be a feeling that we have got it all there (Mark's, with Matthew's, and Luke's and John's extra bits) but we end up without any overview, except what we bring to it ourselves. For in later centuries the death of Jesus was seen, above all, as an act of salvation – he died *for* us. This is not, however, the perspective of the evangelists and, to the extent that we read later beliefs into their Gospels, we misrepresent and misunderstand them.

SYNOPTIC PARABLES

New Testament parables are found only in the Synoptic Gospels, and most of them in Matthew and Luke. Mark has just two parables of any length (the Sower and the Vineyard), two short ones (the Seed growing secretly and the Householder), three very short ones (the Lamp, the Measure, and the Mustard Seed) and four similes (the Old Coat and Wine-skin, the Divided Kingdom, What goes into and comes out of a Man's Mouth, and the Fig Tree). All the Synoptic parables are listed in tables at the end of this chapter. John's Gospel has no parables at all.

Today we tend to think of parables as stories, but the word is used in the Gospels to include similes and wise sayings. In Greek, *parabole* means literally "to throw beside" and so can refer to any illustration or parallel. Michael Goulder has defined it as "a comparison between things divine and human in the form of a story, however slight". Some stories can be very slight. There are also five parables in the Old Testament, although many in later Judaism, and the New Testament parables are written in this same Rabbinic style.

Traditionally all the Gospel parables have been referred to as the "Parables of Jesus". It is an obvious initial assumption, since they are all attributed to him, and those in Mark's Gospel may indeed be his. But it is difficult to be sure and the view will be taken in this chapter that those in Matthew's and Luke's Gospels were written by *them*. So Mark's are our primary parables. Matthew has glossed some of these, copying them out more or less faithfully, but introducing subtle changes to point up the story. Sometimes, however, he adds parables, perhaps to make a pair (as in the parable of the Yeast), or to draw out the meaning of a saying which is unclear (as in the parable of the Labourers in the Vineyard). But faithfulness to Mark is a characteristic of all Matthaean parables. Matthew wrote them, but he did not make them up. He found them in Mark, whether the parable itself or the inspiration for it. As a Christian Scribe, Matthew saw his role as being to amplify and explain his Markan text, and not merely to copy it. Luke is less faithful. He has retained most of the parables in Mark and Matthew, but has rearranged the Matthaean parables and has added others of his own, looking to the Old Testament and Apocrypha for inspiration.

Parables, then, are stories or wise sayings with a moral or message, in which there is a correspondence between details in the parable and aspects of real life, and we see the moral as we register the correspondence. Theoretically *every* detail could be referential and represent something, but in practice such parables are all but impossible to write. In any case, they would make very poor stories. Incidental detail is necessary to make a parable interesting. Mark and Matthew's parables (Matthew's in particular) are highly allegorical. Luke's are much less so, and are better stories in consequence.

Mark's Parables

Mark has just the two parables of any length, the Sower (Mark 4. 3-9, 13-20) and the Vineyard (Mark 12. 1-12). Matthew and Luke include them both and in the Markan order. Whatever further material they added, each regarded Mark's Gospel as the matrix for his own.

Both of these longer Markan parables are highly allegorical and, indeed, the Sower is followed by an explanation of the allegory. So the seed is the Gospel. The Sower is Jesus himself. Three groups of people, who fail to respond to that Gospel for different reasons, are represented by the footpath, the rocky ground, and the thistles. The single group, who do respond to the Gospel, are represented by the good soil. In the same way, in the second of these two parables, the Vineyard is Israel and its owner is God. The vine-growers, the tenants of the vineyard, are the Jewish people. The servants who are sent to represent the owner of the vineyard are the prophets, and the owner's son, who is sent when the servants are rejected, is Jesus. The reckoning, when the tenants are dispossessed and the vineyard given to others, represents God's rejection of Israel and the handing over of the Jewish inheritance to the church. Both of these parables are illustrative of Mark's view that the Jews were destined to reject Jesus. This outcome was assisted by the secrecy with which Mark believed Jesus to have concealed his true identity (the so-called Messianic Secret, which is explained in the chapter on the Gospel according to Mark). It was confirmed by texts such as that which Mark has Jesus quote at the end of the parable of the Vineyard: "The stone, which the builders rejected, has become the main cornerstone...." (Psalm 118. 22-23). Their rejection was predicted in Scripture.

Matthew's Parables

As we would expect, since he wrote them, Matthew's parables are characteristic of his Gospel as a whole and most of them occur in the five discourses. He inherited two of these discourses from Mark and wrote three of his own (the discourses are identified and explained in the chapter on the Gospel according to Matthew).

Allegory helps hearers and readers to interpret a story but, when pressed to extremes, makes the story itself implausible. For all its allegory Mark's parable of the Sower remains convincing as a story, but the Vineyard does not. The moral is completely clear, but it is unlikely in real life that rent collectors would be beaten and killed. Matthew's parables, too, often break down as believable stories through an excess of allegory. In the real world someone who comes to a wedding inappropriately dressed, and particularly when only invited at the last moment, as in the parable of the Wedding Feast (Matthew 22. 1-14), is not normally bound hand and foot and sent to "the place of wailing and grinding of teeth"! In fact this is the standard Matthaean penalty. It is the fate of the lazy servant who does nothing with his talents in the parable of the Talents (Matthew 25. 14-30), and of the goats, who fail to feed the hungry and so forth, in the parable of the Sheep and the Goats (Matthew 25. 31-46). Only Matthew sends his victims to hell, never Mark or Luke.

Many of Matthew's parables also fail as stories through repetition. In the parable of the Talents the man who has been abroad has the identical conversation with the two servants who have been given five and two talents. Each is told "Well done, my good and trusty servant! You have proved trustworthy in a small way; I will now put you in charge of something big. Come and share your master's delight"

(Matthew 25. 14-30). The repetition adds to our sense of foreboding for the third servant with the single talent, who has done nothing with it, but normal conversations are not usually replicated in this way. It is, however, Matthew's style and is common to many of his parables. In the parable of the Houses built on sand and rock, the storm which beats upon each in turn is identically described: "The rain came down, the floods rose, the wind blew, and beat upon that house...." (Matthew 7. 24-27). In some ways it is like a story for children, where a child learns the words in question and repeats them when they recur. But while Matthew's parables lose credibility *as stories* by such repetition, they gain in clarity and conviction. He has an urgent message and all that matters is that the message should be clearly and unequivocally spelt out. It is also always a simple message. There are only ever two options, and where Matthew re-tells a Markan parable which has more, he reduces them to two by glossing. So, in the parable of the Sower, Mark's four outcomes are reduced to two. There are, on the one hand, the three who "hear the word that tells of the Kingdom *but fail to understand it*" and, on the other, the man who "hears the word *and understands it*" (Matthew 13. 18-23). For Matthew, it is a matter of understanding, or not.

One feature that distinguishes Matthew's parables from Luke's is their scale. Kings feature prominently. Matthew's parable of the Wedding Feast (Matthew 22. 1-14) is about a king who prepares a banquet for his son's wedding. Luke retains references to the wedding in his preamble, but the meal itself, when we come to it, is just a dinner party (Luke 14. 7-24). And where Matthew's king has large numbers of servants, the host at Luke's dinner party has just one, who amusingly has to do on his own all that the king's many servants did together in Matthew's parable. He has a busy time, but such anomalies can arise when you gloss someone else's story. Again, Matthew's parable of the Talents (Matthew 25. 14-30; Luke 19. 11-27) is about a man of amazing wealth, for even a single talent is a vast sum of money (the New English Bible, rather loosely, translates "bags of gold"). Luke, characteristically, scales things down, and the ten servants in his re-write of the parable are only given a *mna* (equivalent to 100 *drachma* and translated *pound* in the New English Bible).

Sometimes Matthew's sources will be clear. When he breaks off for his third discourse (for Hanukkah) at Matthew 18.1, he has just reached Mark 9.50. The verse ends, "Have salt in yourselves; and *be at peace with one another*." So that will be the theme of Matthew's discourse. It is about caring for Christ's "little ones", recovering those who stray, reconciling those who quarrel and warning those who are unforgiving themselves. Matthew will also have had the saying of Jesus at Mark 11.29 in mind: "If you have a grievance against anyone, forgive him, so that your Father in heaven may forgive you the wrongs you have done." He has already drawn on this verse in constructing the Lord's Prayer (Matthew 6.12) and now he will illustrate it with the parable of the Two Debtors (Matthew 18. 23-35). Knowing Matthew's mind, the parable almost writes itself. He will construct a story about a man who is unforgiving, yet needs forgiveness himself. And since Matthew has always thought of sins as debts, let the story be of two debtors. God will be represented as a king (how else?) and the first man's debt, ten thousand talents (an almost unimaginable sum of money). There need be no attempt at characterization (stock characters will be sufficient) and the conversation can be duplicated (each debtor says, when confronted with his debt, "Be patient with me, and I will pay you"). And, finally, what more appropriate punishment for the unforgiving debtor (this is a Matthaean parable) than torture. It could have been worse! But Matthew almost certainly also had an Old Testament source in mind, for in Genesis 4 there is another story of brotherly conflict (Cain and Abel), where an unforgiving spirit leads to murder. Lamech, their father, says afterwards to his wives, "Cain may be avenged seven times, but Lamech seventy seven" (in the Greek Old Testament, the Septuagint, "seventy times seven"). And with these same words Jesus answers Peter's enquiry about the limits to forgiveness in the preamble to the parable (Matthew 18. 21-22). Christian forgiveness is limitless.

Matthew's creativity can also be seen in the two little parables of the Buried Treasure and the Pearl of Great Price (Matthew 13. 44-46). Since neither can be found in Mark, we begin to look elsewhere for Matthew's sources. But this is mistaken. We need look no further than Mark 10.21, where Jesus tells the rich stranger, "Go, *sell everything you have*, and give to the poor, *and you will have riches (treasure) in heaven*". For what is the kingdom of God but *hidden* treasure (Mark 4.22)? Matthew rarely deserts Mark and the parable of the Pearl of Great Price simply makes a pair with the Buried Treasure. Each requires the sacrifice of everything else if we are to possess them. Yet their desirability is such that any sacrifice is a matter of sheer joy.

Luke's Parables

Luke's Gospel, too, is a re-write of Mark's and, like Matthew, he also includes the Markan parables, and in order (for the most part) – the Sower, the Lamp, the Measure, the Vineyard, and the Fig Tree. But Luke, perhaps even more than Matthew, is remembered for his parables and they occur, not in discourses as Matthew's do, but in the course of the so-called Lukan Journey (Luke 9.51 – 18.14). This is the Catechism or instruction on the Christian life, which Luke inserts into his Markan matrix and is explained in more detail in the chapter on the Gospel according to Luke. It is the section in his Gospel where he has left himself free to do his own thing and a list of the many parables in this section will be found in the second table at the conclusion of this chapter.

Above all, Luke's parables are memorable and it is in part because they are less allegorical than Mark's and Matthew's. Mark's parable of the Sower is, of course, well known too, but asked to name some of the parables of Jesus many people would begin with the Prodigal Son, or the Pharisee and the Publican. These are both Lukan parables and the stories immediately hold our attention, when they are read as lessons. They are gift texts for preachers. Why, then, is this so?

There *is* more incidental detail, but perhaps most importantly Luke invites us to *identify* with the characters in his parables. They soliloquize and invite us to think with them how they should respond to the particular circumstances in which they find themselves. The prodigal son does this as he "comes to his senses", far from home in a distant country (Luke 15.17). He reviews his options and we review them with him. In the same way the dishonest bailiff *says to himself,* "What am I to do now that my employer is dismissing me?" (Luke 16. 3-4). They almost ask for our advice and we feel qualified to give it, since Luke's characters are not kings, but ordinary people like ourselves, women as well as men, the middle classes, travellers, neighbours, parents, widows, children, businessmen, provincial judges, tax gatherers, Pharisees, Priests and Levites. Luke's congregation would have met people such as these and Luke will have wanted them to think what *they* would have done if they had come across someone who had been assaulted, or had a son who had left home, or who were faced with bankruptcy, or wanted something from a neighbour who had gone to bed, or found that they had more produce than they could possibly store (as in the parable of the Rich Fool). Luke's parables deal with everyday situations and are inherently interesting. They are not mini-parables, like Matthew's Buried Treasure, but proper stories and about all sorts of things (money, prayer, penitence, compassion, humility).

The parables of the Good Samaritan and the Prodigal Son have already been briefly expounded in the chapter on the Gospel according to Luke and others have already been touched on. All Luke's parables are memorable but, short of expounding them all, just two more must suffice to illustrate his style. They follow one another at the beginning of Luke 18 and are about prayer. Luke's source in the first of these, the parable of the Unjust Judge (Luke 18. 1-8), is the Wisdom of Jesus ben Sirah, or Ecclesiasticus (Church Book) as it was called by Christians, since they often used it. Ecclesiasticus 35. 12-17 reminds its readers that God is a just judge. He does not accept bribes, and "has no favourites at the poor man's expense, but listens to his prayer when he is wronged". "He never ignores the appeal of the orphan or the widow when she pours out her complaint. How the tears run down widow's cheeks, and her cries accuse the man who caused them!" So in real life justice can never be relied upon, since judges are rarely completely impartial and favour their own. One's only recourse in such circumstances is patience and persistence. Luke knew of such judges as well and in the parable urged his readers to follow the example of the widow and "keep on praying and never lose heart". God listens to people such as her and will vindicate them.

So persistence is important, but so too is penitence. This is another very common Lukan theme, which he now expounds in the parable of the Pharisee and the Publican (Luke 18. 9-14). Luke had earlier contrasted the penitence of the woman who was living an immoral life and interrupted a dinner party to wash and anoint Jesus' feet, with Simon the Pharisee, his host, who had done nothing similar for him (Luke 7. 36-50). He had told the parables of the Lost Sheep, the Lost Coin, and the Lost Son. Now he will contrast a Pharisee and a tax-gatherer at prayer. But although ostensibly praying, the Pharisee is effectively soliloquizing as he reflects upon his life. He is doing what all Lukan heroes and villains do, which is to tell us about himself and his thoughts. The Publican follows and his prayer and body language, too, all illustrate his penitence. Where Matthew favours the invitation and the warning ("Do this, or else"), Luke is consistently interested in our inner thoughts and motivation. For him the secret of the Christian life is to understand "the mind of Christ" and, to this end, he has Jesus himself soliloquize in the Passion Narrative.

Finally, it is worth noting how diverse are Luke's parables and how carefully ordered. For the Lukan Journey is a Christian instruction and there are many topics to be covered. Uniquely he even gathers the parables together by subject matter. So Luke 15 is concerned with penitence, Luke 16 (The Dishonest Bailiff and Dives and Lazarus) with money, and now Luke 18 with prayer.

So this study shows how the Synoptic Gospels all portray Jesus as teaching primarily in parables, and how Matthew and Luke each construct parables in their own style from the material that lay to hand. So far from being mindless editors (the supposition of those who make them dependent upon written sources such as M, L, Q and the like), they are Christian Scribes, evangelists of absolute genius. And it is difficult, if not impossible, to envisage the Christian Gospel and inheritance without their parables.

Sources: *The Parables of Jesus* by J.Jeremias, published in the 1950s, was regarded as the standard commentary on the parables for many years. Michael Goulder's first article on the parables, "Characteristics of the Parables in the Several Gospels", appeared in the April 1968 issue of the *Journal of Theological Studies*. More was to follow in his *Midrash and Lection in Matthew* (SPCK 1974) and *Luke, a new Paradigm* (Sheffield Academic Press 1989).

The Markan and Matthaean Parables

	Mark	*Matthew*
The two Houses		7. 24-27
The old Coat and Wine-skin	2. 21-22	9. 16-17
The Divided Kingdom and the Strong Man's House	3. 22-30	12. 25-32
The Sower and its Interpretation	4. 3-9, 13-20	13. 4-9, 18-23
The Lamp	4. 21-23	5. 15-16
The Measure	4. 24-25	13.12
The Seed growing secretly (Matthew: The Tares)	4. 26-29	13. 24-30, 36-43
The Mustard Seed	4. 30-32	13. 31-32
The Yeast		13.33
The Buried Treasure		13.44
The Pearl of Great Price		13.45
The Net full of fish		13. 47-50
What goes into and comes out of a man's mouth	7. 14-23	15. 10-11, 15-20
The Lost Sheep		18. 12-14
The Two Debtors		18. 23-35
The Labourers in the Vineyard		20. 1-16
The Man with two Sons		21. 28-32
The Vineyard	12. 1-11	21. 33-43
The Wedding Feast		22. 1-14
The Fig Tree	13. 28-31	24. 32-35
The Householder	13. 33-37	24. 42-44
The Trusty Servant		24. 45-51
The Ten Bridesmaids		25. 1-13
The Talents		25. 14-30
The Sheep and the Goats		25. 31-46

The Markan and Matthaean parables are shown in a single table since, with one exception (Mark 4. 21-23; cf Matthew 5. 14-16), Matthew retains *all* the Markan parables *and in the same order*. At first sight Mark's parable of the Seed growing secretly (Mark 4. 26-29) appears to have been left out, but closer study shows Matthew to have re-written it as the parable of the Tares. Similarly Matthew first repeats Mark's parable of the Householder, or Man away from home (Mark 13. 33-37) and then goes on to create three further parables from ideas within it - the Trusty Servant, the Ten Bridesmaids and the Talents (Matthew 24.45 - 25.30).

The Lukan Parables

	Luke	Matthew
The Good Samaritan	10. 29-37	
The Friend who calls at midnight	11. 1-13	
The Divided Kingdom and the Strong Man's House	11. 14-23	(12. 25-30)
The Lamp	11. 33-36	
The Rich Fool	12. 13-21	
The Householder and the Trusty Servant	12. 35-48	24.42 - 25.30
The Fig Tree	13. 6-9	
The Mustard Seed	13. 18-19	(13. 31-32)
The Yeast	13. 20-21	13.33
The Wedding Feast	14. 7-11	
The Dinner Party	14. 15-24	
The Man who would build a tower	14. 25-30	
The King who would go to battle	14. 31-33	
The Lost Sheep	15. 1-7	
The Lost Coin	15. 8-10	
The Lost Son, or Prodigal, Son	15. 11-32	21. 28-32
The Dishonest Bailiff	16. 1-13	
Dives and Lazarus	16. 19-31	
The Servant and his Master	17. 7-10	
The Unjust Judge	18. 1-8	
The Pharisee and the Tax-gatherer	18. 9-14	
The Pounds	19. 11-27	25. 14-30

Note: The parables shown in brackets in the Matthaean column were originally Markan parables, but a third column would be needed to show Mark's parables separately. Luke, also, retains almost all Mark's other parables, such as the Sower (Luke 8. 4-15) and the Vineyard (Luke 20. 9-19). But, as can be seen, most of Luke's own parables are found in the Lukan Journey (Luke 9.51 - 18.14).

SYNOPTIC MIRACLES

Miracles are represented as an integral part of the ministry of Jesus in the Synoptic Gospels. Healing miracles predominate, but there are nature miracles as well. Specifically, there are thirteen healing miracle stories in Mark's Gospel, and fourteen each in Matthew's and Luke's. Many of these are common to all three Gospels. Mark and Matthew also have the same four nature miracles and Luke three (two of Mark's and one of his own). These are all listed in tables at the end of the chapter.

It may seem pedantic to count the healing miracles when all three Synoptic Gospels imply that Jesus did many more healing miracles than they describe, but there is evidence that Mark and Matthew themselves counted the miracles and thought the number thirteen significant. Jesus' primary ministry was to Israel and, as Israel of old was based upon the twelve tribes (the descendants of Jacob's twelve sons), the church thought of itself as descended from the twelve disciples. But the church also had a worldwide mission and of Mark's thirteen healing miracles one was of a Gentile[1], the Syro-Phoenician woman's daughter (Mark 7. 24-30). Initially Jesus seems to have been reluctant to heal her on this account, but is persuaded to do so by her mother's insistence. Mark's thirteen healing miracles therefore yield twelve Jewish healings and one Gentile (all Israel, but the wider world as well).

Matthew understood this but in re-writing Mark had some juggling to do. In chapters 8 - 12 he has eleven healing miracle stories (ten Jewish and one Gentile), but he *doubles up* Mark's single demoniac at Matthew 8. 24-30 and has *two* blind men healed at Matthew 9. 27-31. So although he only has eleven healing miracles in this section, he still has twelve Jewish *people* healed and one Gentile (the Centurion's son). Mark's interest in numbers is further illustrated by the importance he attaches to the number of loaves used, and the basketfuls left over, in the two feeding miracles (Mark 8. 14-21). And Matthew is careful to explain the significance of the number of generations in the genealogy at the beginning of his Gospel (Matthew 1.17).

There are many fewer nature miracles. Mark has just four (the two feeding miracles, the stilling of the storm and the walking on the water) and Matthew includes them all. Luke includes just *one* of Mark's two feeding miracles and the stilling of the storm, but also adds one of his own - the miraculous catch of fish. We do well to be cautious, however, in ever concluding that Matthew and Luke have left out Markan stories altogether. Mark's was the matrix for both their Gospels and often, when it seems at first sight that a Markan story has gone missing, we discover that it has been re-written and used elsewhere. So Mark's story of Jesus' walking on the water (Mark 6. 45-52) reappears in Luke's post-resurrection narrative (Luke 24. 36-43). In both stories the disciples are frightened. In both they at first think that Jesus is a ghost, and in both he says to them, "It is I myself", and allays their fears.

As in almost everything else John's Gospel is both different and inscrutable. He prefers to describe the seven miracles in his Gospel as "signs" and the first two are numbered. Three are probably Markan stories, but John's sources are rarely clear.

Mark's Healing Miracles

Mark's Gospel is much the shortest of the three Synoptic Gospels and, since they all have roughly the same number of healing miracles, it follows that they represent a much bigger proportion of his Gospel than they do of the other two. There are two discourses in Mark (chapters 4 and 13), but the story of Jesus' ministry, as he tells it, is dominated by miracles. Mark also tells the miracle stories at much greater length than Matthew and Luke. So the story of the Gerasene demoniac runs to twenty verses in Mark, but only seven in Matthew. The raising of Jairus' daughter and the healing of the woman with haemorrhages (one story inside another) take twenty-seven verses in Mark, just nine in Matthew, and seventeen in Luke. This is a consistent pattern.

Mark's Gospel can therefore seem, particularly in the early chapters, to be largely made up of miracle stories. He has three substantial summaries of Jesus' ministry (Mark 1. 32-34, 3. 7-12 and 6. 53-56) and none of these include any reference to his teaching. Certainly, in Mark's mind, it was the miracles that drew the crowds. It is true that people were astounded at the authority with which he spoke (Mark 1. 21-22), but they responded in much greater numbers to his healing ministry. After Jesus had healed Peter's mother-in-law, "the whole town was there, gathered at the door" (Mark 1. 29-31). Again, in spite of Jesus asking the cleansed leper to tell no one, "people kept coming to him from all quarters" (Mark 1.45). And so it was throughout his ministry. "Wherever he went, to farmsteads, villages, or towns, they laid out the sick in the market places and begged him to let them simply touch the edge of his cloak; and all who touched him were cured" (Mark 6.56). To conclude, therefore, Mark portrays the healing miracles and exorcisms as the main reason why Jesus attracted large crowds.

Mark's summaries do not specify the illnesses for which miraculous healings were sought, but the 13 described in detail fall broadly into three categories - possession by evil spirits, various forms of paralysis, and disability (blindness, deafness, and the inability to speak). Of these, possession by evil spirits is much the most important to Mark and may, in his mind, have been the cause of most illness and disability. Mark's whole Gospel was written in the conviction that Jesus' identity as the Son of God had to be kept secret and the evil spirits, who alone knew the Secret, were therefore his principal initial adversary. Accordingly Jesus goes, armed with God's Spirit and victorious in his contest with Satan (Mark 1. 9-13), to do battle with them. The Scribes, perversely, attribute his ability to exorcise devils to his being in league with them (Mark 3. 22-26), but they do not yet understand the Secret. Nor does Herod, who nevertheless realises that Jesus' miraculous powers are bound up with who he is (Mark 6. 14-16). Many people are saying that he must be a prophet (perhaps Elijah, who also worked miracles) but Herod decides that he is John the Baptist raised from the dead, for he has just executed John and has him on his conscience. But they all are wrong. They are, however, right in thinking that the healing miracles, and exorcisms in particular, are highly significant. They add tremendous tension to Mark's Gospel, as disciples and enemies alike try to come to terms with Jesus' identity.

The Healing Miracles in Matthew and Luke

Mark's Gospel was Matthew's and Luke's principal source and it will never have crossed their minds to do other than include most of Mark's healing miracles. But very little of their *extra* material is miraculous. Matthew adds further discourses and Luke adds the Lukan Journey and so, as a consequence, the miraculous element in their Gospels is diluted. They have roughly the same number of miracle stories as Mark, but they are more briefly told. Their *forte* is parables.

Since Matthew and Luke were so faithful to Mark it was inevitable that many of his references to the Messianic Secret would recur. They glossed some passages of exceptional difficulty, such as Mark 4. 10-12, but they reproduced many others without demur. Nevertheless, Mark's theory of the Messianic Secret was not part of Matthew's or Luke's own understanding of the story of Jesus. Neither of them thought, as Mark did, that Jesus *deliberately* tried to keep his identity secret so that his rejection was inevitable. Rather, they thought of the healing miracles as illustrating and confirming the dawning of a New Age and the coming of God's kingdom. So when John the Baptist sends disciples to ask Jesus whether he is "the one who is to come", Jesus replies, "Go and tell John what you hear and see: the blind recover their sight, the lame walk, the lepers are clean, the deaf hear, the dead are raised to life, the poor are hearing the good news - and happy is the man who does not find me a stumbling-block" (Matthew 11. 2-6). This is a passage that would be out of place in Mark. It is Matthew's lection for Jewish New Year and is a fulfilment of one of the traditional New Year readings: "Then shall the blind men's eyes be opened, and the ears of the deaf unstopped. Then shall the lame man leap like a deer, and the tongue of the dumb shout aloud" (Isaiah 35. 5-6).

The healing miracles, therefore, in both Matthew's and Luke's mind are part of the proclamation of the Gospel, and just as people should have repented at Jesus' preaching, so should they when witnessing his miraculous healings. They were equally compelling. "Alas for you, Chorazin!", Jesus said; "alas for you, Bethsaida! If the miracles that were performed in you had been performed in Tyre and Sidon, they would have repented in sackcloth and ashes" (Matthew 11. 20-24). Tyre and Sidon were Phoenician towns, beyond the scope of Jesus' ministry, yet even they would have responded to his miraculous healings. So, too, would Sodom, a ruined city in Jesus' day and legendary for the severity of God's judgement. Yet Chorazin, Bethsaida, and Capernaum, *Galilean* towns, were unmoved and unrepentant. Luke even sets this passage, albeit somewhat shortened, within the context of the mission of the Seventy-two (Luke 10. 12-15). The healing miracles are, indeed, unmistakable signs that "the kingdom of God has come close" (Luke 10.11).

Elijah and Elisha

For our further understanding of the Synoptic miracles we need to look next to the Old Testament ministries of Elijah and Elisha. Elijah (1 Kings 17 - 2 Kings 2) and Elisha (2 Kings 2 - 13) were, with Samuel, the foremost prophets during the period of the monarchy. Samuel was a contemporary of Saul, while Elijah and Elisha exercised ministries some years later in the early ninth century BC. All three were hugely influential in their own day, and the ministries of Elijah and Elisha, in particular, helped to shape the Synoptic perception of the ministry of Jesus.

Mark and Matthew both thought of John the Baptist as another Elijah. Malachi 4. 5-6, the very last verses of the Old Testament, had promised Elijah's return "before the great and terrible day of the Lord comes", and were thought to have found their fulfilment in John. Matthew twice explicitly identifies Elijah with John. After John's disciples have returned to tell him about Jesus' healing ministry, Jesus tells his own disciples, "John is the destined Elijah, if you will but accept it" (Matthew 11.14). Again, as they descend the mountain after the Transfiguration, Jesus says, "I tell you that Elijah has already come, and they failed to recognise him...". Matthew concludes: "Then the disciples understood that he meant John the Baptist" (Matthew 17. 9-13).

But this identity was implicit from the beginning. Mark describes John as being "dressed in a rough coat of camel's hair, with a leather belt around his waist" (Mark 1.6). This is not just a casual description for those who were interested to know what John looked like, but a *theological* clue. For Elijah was "a hairy man with a leather apron round his waist" (2 Kings 1.8), and "robes of coarse hair" were the uniform of Old Testament prophets (Zechariah 13.4). Many in the crowd, whose views influenced Herod, thought that Jesus himself *was* Elijah. They were wrong, but they were thinking along the right lines (Mark 6. 14-16).

The idea that Mark and Matthew thought of Jesus as another Elisha is less explicit, but very probable. Elisha was Elijah's disciple and successor, and there is the famous story, sometimes read (and with good reason) on Ascension Day, where Elijah ascends to heaven (2 Kings 2. 7-18). Elijah and Elisha come to the River Jordan and, as they cross, Elijah asks Elisha whether he can do any last thing for him. Elisha asks that he may inherit a double portion of Elijah's spirit and is told that he will do so if he actually sees Elijah ascend. He does see him ascend, assumes Elijah's cloak which has fallen to the ground, and immediately repeats the miracle that Elijah had just performed (dividing the waters of the River Jordan so that they could cross on dry ground). On seeing this the prophets from Jericho, who were witnesses to it all, conclude: "The spirit of Elijah has settled on Elisha". The similarities with the story of Jesus' baptism are striking (Mark 1. 1-13). Jesus, too, comes to the River Jordan to be baptised by John. As Elisha inherits a *double* portion, so John tells the crowds: "After me comes one who is mightier than I." As Jesus comes up from beneath the water, he sees (and he alone) the Spirit descending upon him, and hears a voice from heaven. And Jesus' ministry only begins when John's ends in his arrest (Mark 1.14).

Thereafter the ministry of Jesus is Elisha-like in the sense that both performed miracles and indeed, sometimes, similar miracles. 2 Kings 4 describes a succession of Elisha's miracles - the miraculous flow of oil to enable a newly widowed woman to redeem her two sons from slavery (2 Kings 4. 1-7), the miraculous birth of a child to the Shunammite woman with an elderly husband (2 Kings 4. 8-17), the raising of that same child some years later, when it had suddenly and unexpectedly died (2 Kings 4. 18-37), and two miraculous feedings in time of famine (2 Kings 4. 38-41, 42-44). In the same way Jesus had raised Jairus' daughter (Mark 5. 21-24, 35-43) and fed the five thousand (Mark 6. 30-44). The feeding miracles are particularly alike - the disbelief of both Elisha's and Jesus' disciples, the promise that they will all eat, and that some will be left over.

Understanding the Miracle Stories today

A belief in the miraculous still persists within the major Christian denominations today, in some more in theory than in practice, but persists nevertheless. Within the Roman Catholic Church, for example, the first miracle attributable to Mother Teresa of Calcutta since her death has already been reported and so starts the process whereby she will be canonised and made a saint. Within conservative evangelical churches, too, the exorcism of evil spirits from those believed to be possessed by them is still practised through a process known as deliverance, and various other miraculous outcomes are sought in answer to prayer. In some Third World countries, too, where superstition persists, a belief in miracles still has a natural place. Elsewhere, however, there is widespread scepticism. Very few Christians specifically deny the miraculous, but even fewer claim to have had any personal experience of it themselves. By contrast with the Middle Ages, when belief in the miraculous was almost universal, things have gone very quiet indeed.

The wisest course for high profile Christians is to address other issues and, if pressed on the subject of miracles, to be non-committal. For few modern preachers respond enthusiastically when given a miracle story for their text, and sermons on miracle stories are generally marked by evasiveness. Congregations are rarely sure at the end of such sermons whether the preacher actually believes the story himself or not. This Handbook, by contrast, discounts the miraculous altogether and so the need to be defensive. In fact miracle stories have neither to be attacked nor defended, but understood.

Several *un*satisfactory solutions to the problem have been suggested in the past. One is to try to show that events, which were thought to be miraculous at the time, can be explained today in an entirely naturalistic way. So these miracles were never true miracles in the first place, but were only perceived as such. An example of this would be the cure of someone who was thought to be possessed by an evil spirit, but was in fact epileptic. Less convincingly, it could be argued that Jesus never actually walked on the water, but only appeared to do so, or again, that unknown to the disciples, further loaves were found in the two feeding miracles. But naturalistic explanations destroy the integrity of a text. They suggest that the miracles were all a big misunderstanding and this obviously undermines the credibility and authority of the Gospels as a whole. Naturalistic explanations, even where convincing, only solve one problem to create another.

The first New Testament scholar to address the question of miracles was David Friedrich Strauss, whose *Life of Jesus* was published in 1835. It was a very courageous book and remarkably prescient for its time. Strauss was specifically concerned to eliminate the miraculous from the ministry of Jesus and was one of the first, and perhaps the very first, to suggest that some, at least, of the Gospel miracle stories were rewrites of Old Testament stories, along the lines suggested above. But these suggestions were never followed up and, for all the interest that Strauss' book inspired, the church as a whole remained very hostile throughout the nineteenth century to any suggestion that the Biblical miracle stories, whether in the Old Testament or the New, were not literally true. One of the contributors to *Essays and Reviews*[2], which was published in 1860, suggested that Balaam's ass could not actually have spoken (Numbers 22. 28-35) and thereby caused an immense furore, which brought great grief to himself and his fellow contributors.

Today much of the heat has gone out of the debate, although the issue remains unresolved. But the answer, surely, is to accept that the New Testament is a first century book, while we are twenty-first century people. For a thousand reasons (cultural, scientific and philosophical), it is inevitable that we shall see the world very differently than they did. But this does not belittle first century authors. It is inconceivable that the Gospels would not include miracle stories, given their prevalence in the Old Testament. We simply need to accept them as stories, many of them stories pure and simple, and only some with a historical basis. It is never possible to distinguish these two groups absolutely, but where most of the details in any given story can be traced to an Old Testament source it is obviously less likely to have an historical basis.

As explained in the chapter on the Synoptic Gospels, this book is written on the assumption that Mark, Matthew and Luke are successive re-writes of a single Gospel, rather than three independent Gospels with their own sources. We can, therefore, see how Matthew and Luke respond to Mark's miracle stories as they come to them. We have already noticed that there is a general tendency to shorten such stories, indicating that their primary interest lay elsewhere. They do not want to leave out any Markan material, but shortening it is another matter. Or, in some instances, they gloss Mark's stories. So Matthew doubles up Mark's single demoniac and single blind man, as shown in the table at the end of this chapter, not because he knew better, but because it served a *theological* purpose. Matthew and Luke can also seem to add further stories of their own, when on closer study these seemingly *new* stories can again be seen not to be new stories at all, but perhaps composite stories, like Matthew's story of the healing of two blind men (Matthew 9. 27-31), or maybe, yes, a new story, but one whose inspiration Luke has found in Mark and Matthew, like the story of the Miraculous Catch of Fish (Luke 5. 1-11)[3]. Luke asked himself, "How could the disciples follow Jesus to become fishers of men, when they knew so little about him?", and then, by drawing upon seemingly small details in his two master texts, he creates his miracle story to explain how they came to give Jesus their commitment.

This process whereby Matthew and Luke added material of their own is an interesting study in itself, but the relevant point here is that *they* treat Mark's stories as stories. And we can do so as well. Many of them are wonderful stories and it is often possible to make them our starting point in addressing twenty-first century issues, as Matthew and Luke did in the first century.

[1] Gentile is a commonly used word in the New Testament to denote anyone who is not Jewish. Samaritans were an intermediate group, half Jewish and half Gentile, although not recognized by Jewish people as

such. They were the descendants of the Northern Kingdom of Israel, created on Solomon's death, when Jeroboam son of Nebat seceded with the 10 tribes to form a separate kingdom (1 Kings 12. 1-19). This left Judah on its own, the true heir of the Jewish tradition, in the eyes of the Deuteronomic historian, the author of 1 - 2 Samuel and 1 - 2 Kings. Samaria, the capital of Israel, was destroyed by Shalmaneser, king of Assyria, in 722 BC. when the nation lost its identity (2 Kings 18. 9-12). By contrast, when Jerusalem, the capital of the Southern Kingdom of Judah, fell to Nebuchrezzar, king of Babylon, in 586 BC (2 Kings 25), the exiles retained their identity and returned a century or more later to rebuild the city.

[2] *Essays and Reviews*, published in 1860, is a collection of seven essays by, amongst others, Benjamin Jowett, the famous Master of Balliol College, Oxford, and Frederick Temple, who was later to become Archbishop of Canterbury. By today's standards it was a very inoffensive book but at the time was felt to undermine the infallibility of the Bible. Samuel Wilberforce, who was Bishop of Oxford, led the opposition to it, as he had done to the publication of Darwin's *Origin of Species* a year earlier. Two contributors were condemned for heresy and 11,000 clergy were moved to affirm their belief in the inspiration of the Scriptures and in eternal damnation.

[3] Michael Goulder expounds the story of the Miraculous Catch of Fish in detail on pages 316-328 of his *Luke, a new Paradigm, Volume 1* (Sheffield Academic Press 1989).

The Synoptic and Johannine Miracles Listed

The Markan Healing Miracles

		Mark	*Matthew*	*Luke*
1	A man is exorcised of an unclean spirit	1. 21-28		4. 31-37
2	Simon's mother-in-law is healed of a fever	1. 29-31	8. 14-15	4. 38-39
3	The healing of a leper	1. 40-45	8. 1-4	5. 12-16
4	The healing of a paralytic	2. 1-12	9. 2-8	5. 17-26
5	Jesus heals a man with a withered hand	3. 1-6	12. 9-14	6. 6-11
6	The healing of the Gerasene demoniac	5. 1-20	*8. 28-34	8. 26-39
7	The raising of Jairus' daughter	5. 21-24 and 35-43	9. 18-19 and 23-26	8. 40-42 and 49-56
8	The healing of the woman who suffered from haemorrhages	5. 25-34	9. 20-22	8. 43-48
9	Jesus exorcises the Syro-Phoenician woman's daughter	7. 24-30	*15. 21-28*	
10	Jesus heals a man who is a deaf mute	7. 31-37	*15. 29-31*	
11	Jesus heals a blind man	8. 22-26		
12	Jesus heals a man's deaf and dumb son	9. 14-29	*17. 14-21*	9. 37-43
13	Jesus heals blind Bartimaeus	10. 46-52	*20. 29-34*	18. 35-43

*a double healing (Matthew adds a second demoniac). The last four of the Matthaean parallels listed above and printed in italic are not included in his count of 12 + 1. The four stories listed on the next page, however, are.

Matthaean and Lukan Additions

		Matthew	Luke
1	The healing of the Centurion's Son	*8. 5-13	7. 1-10
2	Jesus raises the widow's son to life at Nain		7. 11-17
3	The healing of two blind men	*9. 27-31	
4	The healing of a man who was dumb and possessed by a devil	9. 32-34	
5	Jesus heals a blind and dumb man, who is possessed by a devil	12. 22-24	
6	The healing of a crippled woman on the Sabbath		13. 10-17
7	The healing of a man with dropsy on the Sabbath		14. 1-6
8	The healing of the ten lepers		17. 11-19

* The Healing of the Centurion's Son is Matthew's Gentile healing, and the healing of two blind men is his second double healing.

Summaries of Jesus' Healing Ministry

		Mark	Matthew	Luke
1	The first summary: "That evening after sunset...."	1. 32-34	8. 16-17	4. 40-41
2	A second, shorter summary: "So all through Galilee...."	1.39	4. 23-25	4.44
3	A third summary: "Great numbers from Galilee...."	3. 7-12	12. 15-21	6. 17-19
4	A fourth summary: Jesus' reputation as a miracle worker grows	6. 53-56	14. 34-36	
5	The lame, blind, dumb and crippled are healed		15. 29-31	

The Significance of Jesus' Healing Ministry

		Mark	Matthew	Luke
1	Jesus drives out devils by Beelzebub	3. 22-30	12. 24-32	11. 14-22
2	Jesus meets scepticism in his home town	6. 1-6	13. 53-58	4. 16-30
3	Jesus commissions the disciples to extend his ministry	6. 7-13		9. 1-6
4	Herod thinks that Jesus is John the Baptist raised to life	6. 14-16	14. 1-2	9. 7-9
5	Jesus' message for John the Baptist		11. 2-6	7. 18-23
6	Jesus denounces the impenitence of the towns in which his miracles have been performed		11. 20-24	10. 13-15
7	The demand for a sign - none shall be given		12. 38-42	11. 29-32

The Nature Miracles

		Mark	Matthew	Luke
1	The miraculous draught of fishes			5. 1-11
2	The stilling of the storm	4. 35-41	8. 23-27	8. 22-25
3	The feeding of the five thousand	6. 30-44	14. 13-21	9. 10-17
4	Jesus walks on the Sea of Galilee	6. 45-52	14. 22-33	(24. 36-43)
5	The Feeding of the Four Thousand	8. 1-10	15. 32-39	

John's Seven Signs

1	The changing of water into wine at the wedding in Cana-in-Galilee	2. 1-11
2	The healing of the son of the officer in royal service	4. 46-54
3	The healing of the cripple at the Sheep Pool in Jerusalem on the Sabbath	5. 1-18
4	The feeding of the five thousand	6. 1-13
5	Jesus walks on the Sea of Galilee	6. 16-21
6	The healing of the man who was born blind	9. 1-12
7	The raising of Lazarus	11. 1-44

THE LORD'S PRAYER

The Lord's Prayer, so-called because it is traditionally ascribed to Jesus, is found in two slightly different versions in Matthew 6. 9-13 and Luke 11. 2-4. The prayer can be divided into eleven units:

	Matthew 6. 9-13	*Luke 11. 2-4*
1	Our Father in heaven,	Father,
2	Thy name be hallowed;	Thy name be hallowed;
3	Thy kingdom come,	Thy kingdom come.
4	Thy will be done,	
5	on earth as in heaven.	
6	Give us today our daily bread.	Give us each day our daily bread.
7	(And) forgive us the wrongs we have done (literally, our debts)	And forgive us our sins,
8	as we have forgiven those who have wronged us.	for we too forgive all who have done us wrong.
9	And do not bring us to the test,	And do not bring us to the test.
10	but save us from the evil one.	
11	(For thine is the kingdom and the power and the glory, for ever and ever. Amen.)	

Since the original prayer is in Greek, there can obviously be many different English translations of it and, in fact, the traditional translation of the seventh clause of Matthew's version of the prayer is wrong. Matthew thought of sins as debts and his petition translates, literally, "Forgive us our *debts*". He also represented sins as debts in the Parable of the Two Debtors (Matthew 18. 23-35). But Luke took a different view and his petition is correctly translated.

Mark's Gospel, the first to be written, does not include the Lord's Prayer and he is therefore presumed not to have known it. Matthew's is thought to be the original version of the Prayer and Luke's a shorter version. John wrote last, and can be presumed to have left it out intentionally, since he will have known the other Gospels. Line 11 is a later addition by someone who thought to round the Prayer off. It is not in either Sinaiticus or Vaticanus, two of the three oldest manuscripts.

Where, then, did Matthew get the Lord's Prayer from? Traditionally, from Jesus. But it is puzzling that Mark and John left it out and that Luke shortened it. Would they have dared to do that if Jesus himself was its author? A more likely explanation is that Matthew compiled the Lord's Prayer from the sources that were available to him. His principal source was Mark, but some units were suggested by Old Testament texts.

Matthew's Sources

The most famous occasion on which Jesus prayed was in Gethsemane in the hours immediately before his arrest (Mark 14. 32-42) and they are indeed the only prayers of Jesus that Mark actually quotes. Matthew will therefore obviously want to include them:

"Abba, Father, " Jesus said, "all things are possible to thee; take this cup away from me. *Yet not what I will, but what thou wilt."* This gives us Lines 1 and 4 of the Lord's Prayer (*Abba* is Aramaic for Father). Mark continues: "He came back and found them asleep; and he said to Peter, 'Asleep, Simon? Were you not able to stay awake for one hour? Stay awake all of you and *pray that you may be spared the test.* The spirit is willing but the flesh is weak.'" This gives us Line 9.

Although not a prayer itself, Matthew also found a saying of Jesus *about* prayer at Mark 11.25: "And when you stand praying, *if you have a grievance against anyone, forgive him,* so that *your Father in heaven* may forgive you the wrongs you have done." This supplied Lines 7 and 8, as well as adding "in heaven" to Line 1.

We are left with Lines 2, 3, 5 and 6. "Thy name be hallowed" may have been suggested by the Ten Commandments, of which the Sermon on the Mount is a Christian rewrite. The fourth commandment reads: "You shall not make wrong use of the name of the Lord your God." Matthew prefers to put this more positively. You should hallow, or bless, God's name.

Line 3 draws upon the preaching of Jesus. The whole of his ministry was an attempt to prepare people for the coming of God's kingdom: "From that day forth Jesus began to proclaim the message: 'Repent; for the kingdom of heaven is upon you.'" (Matthew 4.17) So a Christian will pray, with Jesus, for the coming of that kingdom.

Line 5 translates, literally, "as in heaven, so on earth". This is a common Matthaean expression as, for example, earlier in the Sermon at Matthew 5.18, and also at Matthew 11.25 and 24.35.

And, finally, Line 6 was probably suggested by an Old Testament story associated with the Law giving. The tradition was that a golden period of forty years followed the Exodus from Egypt, in which Israel wandered in the Sinai Desert and were fed by God's daily provision of manna (bread). And, quite specifically, they were only to take enough for each day's need. They were not to store it. Matthew will go on to expound this in Matthew 6. 19-34 where we are urged to take each day in turn and to trust in God's provision, like the birds and the lilies. So "Give us *today* our *daily* bread" is the prayer that follows from this.

We can summarise:

	The Lord's Prayer	Source
1	Our Father in heaven,	Gethsemane (Mark 14.36)
2	Thy name be hallowed;	The fourth of the Ten Commandments (Exodus 20.7)
3	Thy kingdom come,	Jesus' preaching (Mark 1.15)
4	Thy will be done,	Gethsemane (Mark 14.36)
5	on earth as in heaven.	A common Matthaean expression (see above)
6	Give us today our daily bread.	The manna (Exodus 16. 13-25) and the Sermon on the Mount (Matthew 6. 25-34)

7 & 8	(And) forgive us the wrongs we have done (literally, our debts), as we have forgiven those who have wronged us.	The Fig Tree (Mark 11. 20-25) and the Parable of the Two Debtors (Matthew 18. 23-35)
9 & 10	And do not bring us to the test, but save us from the evil one.	Gethsemane (Mark 14.38)
11	(For thine is the kingdom and the power and the glory, for ever and ever. Amen.)	Found in none of the oldest manuscripts

Luke's Version of the Prayer

Luke's version of the Prayer is little known and never used. It is shorter and simpler, but has been judged too short. And it is secondary. Matthew's is the original version of the Prayer. He wrote it.

Luke follows the Lord's Prayer with the parable of the Friend who calls at Midnight (Luke 11. 5-13), which expounds Matthew's "Ask, and you will receive; seek, and you will find; knock and the door will be opened" (Matthew 7.7) further on in the Sermon.

The Meaning of the Prayer

So the Lord's Prayer will be seen to have four principal petitions:

> that God's will may be done;
> that he will provide for our needs;
> that he will forgive us; and
> that he will protect us.

Only the last of these calls for comment. This is the prayer that God will not "bring us to the test", which, in the context of Gethsemane, is a prayer that God will spare us unnecessary suffering and will sustain us in life's trials and tribulations. But it had earlier been translated in the Authorized Version of the English Bible, and in the Book of Common Prayer, "Lead us not into *temptation*". This was corrected in the early versions of the

Alternative Service Book 1980 to, "Do not bring us to the time of trial", but it proved unpopular and a majority of people wanted the old version back.

JESUS' FAMILY AND FRIENDS

As Jesus increasingly came to be represented as a divine figure, it was natural that his human family should be overlooked, and eventually denied. Only his mother was depicted with him, and she was accordingly elevated to only a slightly inferior status (immaculately conceived herself, ever-virgin, assumed into heaven with him at her death, and, according to some, co-redemptorix). But the evidence of the New Testament and of Eusebius of Caesarea, the first church historian, is to the contrary. Jesus was one of a large family, some at least of whom were married, and he will have had nephews and nieces. Indeed, there must be many people today who are directly, if distantly, related to him through his brothers and sisters.

His Mother, Mary

Jesus' mother was called Mary. We do not know her father's name or anything further about her family. There is no contemporary evidence to support the belief that her mother was called Anne. Anne is not mentioned in the New Testament and she was only commemorated widely in the Middle Ages. Mary herself is many times referred to by name in the two Birth Narratives (Matthew 1-2 and Luke 1-2), but only twice elsewhere, at Mark 6. 1-6 (Matthew 13. 53-58) and Acts 1.14. She is several times referred to in John's Gospel, but never by name and Jesus himself calls her "Woman" on the two occasions when he addresses her (John 2.4 and 19.26). In John's mind it would seem that Jesus was not so much born, as "came down from heaven".

Mary's husband was called Joseph. They had a large family (see below) and she was a member of the early church (Acts 1.14 again). And that is all we know. But many legends and a huge number of doctrines have grown up around her, some in conflict with these few certain facts.

So the Roman Catholic Church today believes that Jesus was Mary's *only* child, and that he was miraculously conceived without sexual intercourse. He can therefore be thought of as like us in respect of his being human, but unlike us in being free of the original sin, which (in Catholic teaching) sexual intercourse perpetuates. So Mary herself is referred to in the Creeds as "the Virgin Mary", or, in a devotional context, as the "Blessed Virgin Mary" (B.V.M.). Progressively, further titles and honours have been conferred on her ("Star of the Sea", "Queen of Heaven", and so forth).

From the fourth century onwards she was thought of as "Ever-Virgin", again implying that she never had sexual intercourse and that Jesus was her only child. The Third Ecumenical Council, held at Ephesus in 431, went further and officially accorded her the Greek title "*Theotokos*", which means "God-Bearer" (she gave birth to God). A further title, "Mother of God", also gained general acceptance, and by the fifteenth century Mary herself was believed to have been conceived, like Jesus, without sexual intercourse. This belief was formally defined in 1854 as the Doctrine of the Immaculate Conception. More recently still, in 1950, the Doctrine of the Assumption was added, implying that Mary never died a human death but ascended bodily into heaven.

All these beliefs about Mary have been doctrinally, rather than historically, driven. They are held on the basis of what would be appropriate (*a priori* arguments), rather than on the basis of any evidence. Mary has even been thought of as co-mediator with Jesus, but this is still unofficial. Nevertheless, it is difficult to confer too great a dignity upon her, excepting Godhead. And both Jesus and Mary, thus dignified, have become models of the celibate life, and therefore representative of the monastic ideal. Every monk and nun aspires to be like them.

All these images and beliefs are confirmed in the minds of church people today by the liturgy, Renaissance paintings, popular hymns and the traditional crib scene (Jesus, the God-Man, with Mary his mother, and Joseph his guardian, a three-some).

But, as we shall see, Jesus was one of a large family, with brothers and sisters, some of them married. So the celibate scene is entirely dispelled. Jesus had lots of relations (parents, uncles and aunts presumably, certainly married brothers and sisters, with children and, presumably, grandchildren). It is a very different scenario from the traditional one, and the evidence for it is to be found in the New Testament itself.

His Brothers and Sisters

The stories of the Virgin Birth might seem to exclude Jesus having brothers and sisters, but Matthew is not apparently conscious of any contradiction. He presents the Table of Descent as listing Jesus' true paternal descendants, and includes the passages discussed below where Mark makes mention of his brothers and sisters, in both cases without any suggestion of inconsistency. Luke is more meticulous. He introduces his Table of Descent (the names are different, but no matter) with a careful qualification: "When Jesus began his work he was about thirty years old, the son, *as people thought*, of Joseph" (Luke 3. 23-38). It would seem that Luke is aware of the inconsistency, which Matthew has overlooked. But in that case why does he include the Table of Descent at all? It was an impossible problem to resolve. Like Matthew, Luke also knew that Jesus had brothers and sisters, and this may have led him to slip into his birth narrative that Jesus was Mary's *first-born* (Luke 2.7). It leaves it open for her to have other children, as she did, afterwards.

And so to the two principal Markan texts. The first begins: "So his mother and his brothers arrived, and remaining outside sent in a message asking him to come out to them" (Mark 3. 31-35; Matthew 12. 46-50; Luke 8. 19-21). He is told, and replies, "Who is my mother? Who are my brothers?" Looking round at those in the room with him, he says, "Here are my mother and my brothers. Whoever does the will of God is my brother, my sister, my mother." Mark is not concerned to tell us about Jesus' family for its own sake, but they were around and occasionally intrude, sometimes awkwardly, into the story.

The second passage is clearer still. Jesus teaches in the synagogue of his home-town (Mark appears to deliberately avoid calling it Nazareth, although we have already been told that Jesus was known as Jesus of Nazareth) and the large congregation is amazed at his wisdom and ability to perform miracles. They exclaim, "How does he work such miracles? Is not this the carpenter, the son of Mary, the brother of James and

Joseph and Judas and Simon? And are not his sisters here with us?" (Mark 6. 1-6; Matthew 13. 53-58).   This is quite unambiguous and cannot be explained away as a reference to cousins. Mark never uses the word "brothers" (*adelphoi*) in any but a literal sense.

Luke leaves out Mark's second story or perhaps re-writes it at Luke 4. 14-30. Luke begins: "So he came to Nazareth, where he had been brought up, and went to the synagogue on the Sabbath day as he regularly did". He reads from Isaiah 61 and concludes, "Today, in your very hearing, this text has come true". As in Mark's story the congregation are amazed "that words of such grace should fall from his lips. 'Is not this Joseph's son?', they asked." The family is well known, although Luke does not enumerate at this point. He does do so later, however, at the beginning of the Acts of the Apostles. He says that the apostles were "constantly at prayer together, and with them a group of women, including Mary the mother of Jesus, *and his brothers*" (Acts 1.14).

We therefore seem to be on firm ground in assuming that Jesus' parents were, indeed, Joseph and Mary, that he had four brothers (all named) and an unknown number of sisters (who are not named). And we are not to suppose that they were against him - they were among his supporters.

James, the Lord's Brother

James (Jacob) is a common Jewish name and there is a natural confusion between James the son of Zebedee, one of the Twelve, and James the brother of Jesus. But there is an incontrovertible reference to "James the Lord's brother" in Galatians 1.19, and it is important to notice that it is also implied that Paul thinks of him as an apostle as well. It has been maintained by some in the past that only the disciples were apostles, but this is not so, and by the end of the first century the words "disciple" and "apostle" were practically interchangeable. And since this first reference to James in Galatians is to James, the brother of the Lord, it is reasonable to assume that the two subsequent references are to him as well (Galatians 2.9 and 2.12). We also infer that James, the brother of the Lord, was not only an apostle, but a leading apostle. And he was, naturally, a Jewish Christian, to whom Paul was at least partly opposed.

There are also references to James in 1 Corinthians 15.7, and in Acts 12.17, 15.13 and 21.18. These, too, probably refer to James, the Lord's brother, since James, the brother of John, has been beheaded at Acts 12.2. But it is never possible to be absolutely sure, since Luke wants to align the beheading of John the Baptist with the beheading of James, the son of Zebedee, and to describe him as "the brother of John" does this. It serves a theological purpose.

Confirmation of all this is found in Eusebius of Ceasarea's *History of the Church* (Book II, Section 23). Eusebius wrote many years later in the early fourth century, but he always quotes his sources, who in this case are Clement and Hegesippus. Hegesippus wrote: "Control of the church passed to the apostles, together with the Lord's brother James, whom everyone from the Lord's time till our own has called the Righteous (for there were many Jameses)". There were, indeed. And many Marys, too!

The Twelve

The Twelve are listed in each of the Synoptic Gospels, although the lists are not completely consistent (Mark 3. 13-19; Matthew 10. 2-4; Luke 6. 12-16). However, surprisingly little is known about them and most do not feature individually in the story of Jesus at all. The choice of Twelve would be symbolical, since Israel of old was founded on Jacob's twelve sons, the patriarchs.

We do, however, know that some of the disciples were married. We can deduce this from the story of the healing of Peter's mother-in-law (Mark 1. 29-31) and from 1 Corinthians 9. 1-12. This last is a particularly interesting passage. Paul is claiming recognition as an apostle and continues: "To those who put me in the dock this is my answer: Have I no right to eat and drink? Have I no right to take a Christian wife about with me, like the rest of the apostles *and the Lord's brothers*, and Cephas[1]? Or are Barnabas and I alone bound to work for our living?" I conclude that Paul was not married, but that the apostles and brothers of Jesus were, and that their wives (and children?) travelled with them on their journeys. This is all very different indeed from how it was subsequently seen in the mediaeval church.

Jesus' Family in John's Gospel

As in other things, John's Gospel stands apart from the other three in its understanding of Jesus' family relationships. In fact, if we relied upon John's Gospel alone, as many Pauline Christians will have done, we would not even know that Jesus' mother and father were called Mary and Joseph. And although John refers to "the Twelve", he does not list them. It was all a rather delicate matter as far as Pauline Christians were concerned, since their man (Paul) was not one of the Twelve.

Another strange thing about John's treatment of Jesus' family is the way that Jesus twice addresses his mother as "Woman" (John 2.4 and 19. 25-27). The New English Bible translators thought this so strange that they translated it "Mother", without any warrant for doing so. But for John, as for all Pauline Christians, Jesus was the Second Adam (Romans 5. 12-21 and 1 Corinthians 15. 45-49) and the Creation Stories always lie just beneath the surface. So possibly (his mind is often difficult to read) John thinks of Jesus as the Adam figure to his mother's Eve. She was "the Woman" in that sense.

An Uncle?

Eusebius is again interesting (Book III, Section 11) with regard to Cleopas: "After the martyrdom of James and the capture of Jerusalem which instantly followed, there is a firm tradition that those of the apostles and disciples of the Lord who were still alive assembled from all parts together with those who, humanly speaking, were *kinsmen of the Lord* - for most of them were still living. Then they all discussed together whom they should choose as a fit person to succeed James, and voted unanimously that Simeon, son of the Clopas *mentioned in the Gospel narrative*, was a fit person to occupy the throne of the Jerusalem see. He was, so it is said, a cousin of the Saviour, for Hegesippus tells us that Clopas was Joseph's brother". Eusebius actually quotes Hegesippus to this effect later at Book IV, Section 22. So was this Clopas the Cleopas of Luke 24.18? Eusebius says so, and it has to be possible.

Conclusion

Our conclusion is that Jesus, although unmarried himself, was part of a large family and had many married brothers and sisters, as well as nephews and nieces. His disciples, for the most part, were also married men. But in time, all of this seemed inconsistent with the church's belief that Jesus was a uniquely divine figure.

Further, if the monastic ideal represented the highest form of Christian discipleship, as it came to do, it was unhelpful to portray the church's founders, and Jesus' closest disciples, as married men. They must surely have been celibate as well.

So today, as a result of Biblical scholarship, Jesus is re-emerging from beneath centuries of doctrine and devotion. And now, too, with him, re-emerge his brothers and sisters, and their children, to form a normal family group.

[1] Peter is known, identified, or referred to, in the New Testament by five different names. They are Simon, Simon Peter, Simon son of John, Peter, and Cephas.

Simon, which has no relevant Greek derivation, would seem to have been his true, first name, and in the Synoptic Gospels is the name by which Jesus himself addresses Peter, when he speaks directly to him (as, for example, at Mark 14.37, Matthew 17.25 and Luke 22.31). Son of John (bar Jonah) is the Jewish equivalent of his surname and is used only once.

Peter (from the Greek *petros*, meaning a "stone") is the name by which the Synoptic evangelists most commonly refer to him and, they imply, is a name that Jesus himself gave Peter, whether when he was first called (Mark 3.16 and Luke 6.14) or at Caesarea Philippi (Matthew 16. 16-20). They never use the name Cephas, which is a word of Syriac derivation, but of similar meaning.

Only Paul consistently uses the name Cephas for Peter, and John's, a Pauline Gospel, explains how Jesus gave him this name at John 1. 40-42. His own preferred way of referring to Peter, however, is Simon Peter.

THE EMPTY TOMB

Since appeal is so often made to the story of the Empty Tomb in any discussion of the resurrection, it deserves particularly careful analysis. I write this after the recent announcement of the appointment of a senior churchman, when almost the first question he was asked was whether he believed in the bodily resurrection of Jesus. He did. So there was no need to press him further. For today the story of the Empty Tomb has become a test of Christian orthodoxy. Any failure to affirm it positively, any prevarication, can lead to charges of heresy. So most Christian leaders, with the occasional honourable exception, choose not to discuss the story of the Empty Tomb in public. It may even be that some readers, finding this chapter in the Table of Contents, will turn to it first.

It is important to note, first of all, that no reference to the story of the Empty Tomb is made in any of Paul's Letters. For Paul the primary evidence for the resurrection of Jesus was his appearance to the disciples after his death and, even more importantly than that, his own experience of encountering the risen Jesus on the road to Damascus. He lists these resurrection appearances (to them and to him) in 1 Corinthians 15. 1-11, and as his Letters pre-date the Gospels, it is clear that Pauline Christians believed in the resurrection of Jesus *independently of the story of the discovery of the Empty Tomb.*

For reasons given elsewhere, this study will also assume that Mark's Gospel was written first, that Matthew's Gospel is a re-write of Mark's, and that Luke's Gospel conflates them. There will therefore be no attempt, as in Frank Morrison's *Who moved the stone?*[1], to reconcile the four accounts as if they were the reports of four individual eye-witnesses, which they are not. Rather, reasons will be suggested for the glosses and additions, which each evangelist has made.

The Original Story – Mark's

I need, first, to summarise Mark's story (Mark 16. 1-8) as an aide-mémoire. Three women, then, Mary of Magdala, Mary the mother of James, and Salome, come to the tomb early on the

Sunday morning to anoint the body of Jesus. They are surprised to find that the stone, which they thought would block the entrance, has already been rolled back. They enter and find a young man in a white robe, who tells them that Jesus has risen, that his body is no longer there, and that they are to tell the disciples that he will go before them into Galilee. But the women are frightened, run away, and say nothing to anybody.

What then were Mark's sources for this story? There can be no certain answer, but they are often found in the Old Testament and perhaps, in this case, in the Books of Joshua and Daniel. Joshua tells the story of the Jewish conquest of Palestine, and chapter 10 describes how five defeated kings seek refuge in a cave at Makkedah (Joshua 10. 16-27). It is a gruesome story. When the kings are taken prisoner and held in the cave, Joshua instructs his men to "roll some great stones to the mouth of the cave and post men there to keep watch". He leaves and returns later, when the kings are brought out again. Joshua says to the Israelites, "Do not be fearful or dismayed; be strong and resolute; for the Lord will do this to every enemy you fight against". He then beheads the kings, and their bodies are "hung on five trees, where they remained hanging until evening". At sunset they are taken down and their bodies thrown back into the cave. "They piled great stones against its mouth, and there the stones are to this day".

Mark, obviously, would not think to identify Jesus with the five kings, and the outcome of his entombment will be very different from theirs. But his body, too, is taken from the cross at dusk, "laid in a tomb cut out from the rock", and a stone rolled against the entrance. But where the stones in Joshua's story are "there to this day", the women found that the stone, which had sealed Jesus' tomb, huge though it was, had been "rolled back already". It is a powerful expression of Mark's conviction that Jesus, the Son of God, has risen from the dead and, if not this year then perhaps next, will return in glory. The youth in a white robe also says to the women, *"Fear nothing; you are looking for Jesus of Nazareth..."*, which echo Joshua's words, *"Do not be fearful or dismayed..."*.

The case would be strengthened if a reason could be shown why Mark might have had this text in mind and there is, indeed, a possible explanation. Mark's Passion Narrative will have been read in Christian Jewish synagogues over Passover, which falls at the end of the second or third week in Nisan. The story of the Empty Tomb will, therefore, have been read on the second or third Sabbath of the liturgical year. And if the Book of Joshua were the Haphtarah (second reading), Mark's story would more or less fall against Joshua 10 and could be regarded as a fulfilment of it. It provides both the setting for Mark's story and its moral ("Do not be afraid").

Classically, midrash conflates two or more stories to produce something new and original, and Mark, too, had such a second source in the Book of Daniel. We know that it will have been fresh in his mind because of the many references to it in the Passover Discourse (Mark 13). Daniel was written in a time of conflict to provide encouraging examples of heroic endeavour (Daniel 1 - 6) and to hold out, in a series of visions, the promise that the end of the world was imminent (Daniel 7 - 12). The last vision is particularly pertinent in prophesying *a general resurrection*. After the time of distress Michael will appear; "your people will be delivered, everyone who is written in the book: many of those who sleep in the dust of the earth will wake, some to everlasting life and some to the reproach of eternal abhorrence" (Daniel 12. 1-2).

Earlier stories may also have been in Mark's mind. When Daniel is thrown into the lions' pit, the king tells him, "Your own God, whom you serve continually, will save you". "*A stone was brought and put over the mouth of the pit, and the king sealed it with his signet...*" (Daniel 6.17). Next morning Daniel was found safe and unharmed. "No trace of injury was found in him, because he had *put his faith in God.*" (Daniel 6.23).

Later, Daniel receives another vision from the man clothed in linen: "I, Daniel, alone saw the vision, while those who were near me did not see it, but *great fear fell upon them and they stole away.*" (Daniel 10.7). This latter sentence is particularly interesting as it suggests a further reason why Mark may have had the women "run away from the tomb, beside themselves with terror" and say nothing to anybody.

Other texts than these were almost certainly in Mark's mind and could account for further details, but it would over-complicate things to include them all here. And, in any case, none of this *proves* anything, or is intended to do so. In the absence of historical sources, it simply suggests what may have been in Mark's mind. And the story is not even crucial as far as he was concerned – it was a postscript to his Gospel. Meanwhile it remains to inquire what the other evangelists made of Mark's story.

Matthew's Re-write

Matthew made a number of significant changes. From his point of view Mark's story was highly defective and he addresses its weaknesses in turn[2].

First of all he adds a second, violent earthquake and has an angel descend from heaven to roll the stone from the entrance to the tomb. He had, earlier, introduced an earthquake and general resurrection at the *death* of Jesus (Matthew 27. 50-54) and the addition of the angel and the second earthquake explains, what had been left unexplained in Mark's story, how the stone had been rolled away. An angel had done it. And, like "the man clothed in linen" (Daniel 10. 5-6), the angel's face, too, "shone like lightning" (Matthew 28.3). So where Mark introduces the resurrection of Jesus as a *fait accompli*, Matthew describes it.

Matthew's second addition is the setting of the guard and their subsequent flight (Matthew 27. 62-66 and 28. 11-15). He almost certainly understood Mark better than we do and knew Mark's sources for the story of the Empty Tomb. And if Joshua "posted men at the entrance to the cave to keep watch" (Joshua 10.18), Matthew will supply a guard as well. Like Judas, too, who had been bribed to betray Jesus, the guard are persuaded to accept a bribe from the chief priests to reward their silence and to persuade them to suggest that the resurrection of Jesus was fraudulent. Matthew's instinct is never to discard Mark, whatever the problems his text presents, and he will defend the story. So the setting of the guard guarantees the truth of Mark's principal assertion that the tomb was empty and that Jesus had risen. But it is unlikely that Matthew had access to an independent historical source for this, since there is no evidence of his having one. Matthew always turned to the Old Testament for his inspiration and he found it in the very text which had provided Mark's original starting point.

Mark's story had two further weaknesses, which a Christian Scribe must do what he can to correct. Mark's final verse describes how the two women "ran away from the tomb, beside themselves with terror. They said nothing to anyone, for they were afraid" (Mark 16.8). In Matthew's view this just could not have been true. So he retained the "fear" (using the noun rather than the verb) but added "and with great joy": "They went out from the tomb quickly" (he does not say that they "fled", as Mark had done) "with *fear and great joy*". And they did what they had been told.

But Mark's ending was unsatisfactory in yet another respect, since Jesus promises "to go before the disciples into Galilee", yet never does so. Matthew therefore determines to rectify this omission as well. He has Jesus appear to the disciples on a mountain in Galilee. And as Mark, earlier in his Gospel, had Jesus tell his disciples to proclaim the Gospel to all nations (Mark 13.10), so Matthew will have him do this now. It results in a triumphant conclusion, not just to the Passion narrative, but to Matthew's Gospel as a whole (Matthew 28. 16-20). Those in the early church who looked for a stronger conclusion than Mark's, could not have wished for more.

Luke's Version of Mark's Story

Luke, like Matthew, integrates Mark's story into his Resurrection Narrative, but does not follow Matthew in the glosses and additions he makes. So Mark's "young man in white" becomes, not Matthew's "angel of the Lord", but "*two men* in dazzling garments". Luke believed in angels, but these were not angels but men, and we can establish their probable identity. For it seems very likely indeed that he intended them to be Moses and Elijah, who had been the witnesses of Jesus' transfiguration (Luke 9. 28-36), and would later be the witnesses of his ascension (Acts 1. 9-11).

At the transfiguration Luke alone specifically calls them "men", and explains: "These were Moses and Elijah, who appeared in glory and spoke of his *departure*, the destiny he was to fulfil in Jerusalem" (Luke 9. 28-36). Luke is again deploying his favourite metaphor of life as a journey. Jesus' departure is his death and he will complete that journey into heaven at his ascension, when these same two men, surely, although again not specifically identified, will stand on either side (Acts 1. 9-11). All three instances (the transfiguration, the resurrection, and the ascension) are moments of revelation in which the destiny of Jesus is revealed, a destiny envisaged by Scripture. For as well as representing the two divisions of the Old Testament, the Law and the Prophets, which Jesus fulfilled, both Elijah and Moses had also themselves ascended, as Jesus was about to do. The ascension of Elijah is described in 2 Kings 2. 1-18, and the ascension of Moses in the Assumption of Moses[3].

We come next to what the two men say. And here Luke, ever the great teacher, cannot resist a little revision. So he has the two men tell the women, "*Remember* what he told you while he was still in Galilee, about the Son of Man: how he must be given up into the power of sinful men and be crucified, and must rise again on the third day." "Then they *recalled* his words...." (Luke 24. 6-9).

The testimony of the same two men at Jesus' ascension is also characteristically Lukan. They ask, "Why stand there looking up into the sky? This Jesus, who has been taken away from you up into heaven, will *come* in the same way as you have seen him *go*." (Acts 1.11). It is the metaphor of life as a journey yet again. The first journey was to Jerusalem. The second journey, his departure, was to heaven. And the third journey will be his return, which Luke, like Mark and Matthew, awaited.

Finally Luke, like Matthew, needed to do something about Mark's unsatisfactory ending. In fact, he has a longer and much better ending in mind (Luke 24. 13-53), and at this point simply has the women report the message of the two men to the disciples. In his mind they must surely have done that, whatever Mark said. And he leaves out Mark's unfulfilled promise that Jesus will go before the disciples into Galilee. For Luke, Jerusalem was the focus of the church's activity and it is in Jerusalem and not Galilee that he has the church gather (Acts

1. 12-14). Galilee gets a dutiful mention in Luke's story of the Empty Tomb, but its relevance lies in the past rather than the future.

John's Version of Mark's Story

John dispenses with Mark's "young man wearing a white robe" altogether. Mary of Magdala comes alone to the tomb, unaccompanied by any other Mary, and sees only that the tomb is empty (John 20. 1-9). So she tells "Simon Peter and the other disciple, the one whom Jesus loved". Thereafter the story becomes competitive. The "other disciple" outruns Peter, but Peter is first into the tomb. He sees the linen wrappings and the napkin, but it is the other disciple, "who had reached the tomb first", who also believes first.

The key to the understanding of John's story lies in the identification of "the disciple whom Jesus loved", as explained in the chapter on the Gospel according to John. John intends those who know (that is, Pauline Christians) to believe that Paul, their apostle, comprehensively out-performs Peter. The misunderstanding would undermine any claim which might be made for the historicity of John's story, but we have already seen that Mark's story is itself a midrash of Old Testament texts and so not historical either. The additions which Matthew and Luke make either address problems in Mark, or amplify his text, or align the story with their own distinctive understanding of the life of Jesus as a whole.

[1] *Who moved the Stone?* by Frank Morrison (first published in the 1920s but still available in paperback today).

[2] Scholars are referred to Michael Goulder's *Midrash and Lection in Matthew* (SPCK. 1974), pages 447-449.

[3] Little is known of the Assumption of Moses and the full text has not survived. But it is referred to by ancient authors and may date from the first century AD. Its title speaks for itself.

THE SERMON ON THE MOUNT

The Sermon on the Mount, as we call it today, is the first of five discourses in Matthew's Gospel (Matthew 5 - 7). The New English Bible translation begins: "When Jesus saw the crowds he went up the hill." Sunday School pictures by the likes of Elsie Anna Woods show Jesus, seated on a grassy knoll, talking to a small group of disciples, while children pick wild flowers and chew grass stalks. But Matthew had neither a hill nor a mount in mind, but a mountain, and specifically Mount Sinai. Or, to put it more succinctly, the mountain that Matthew has Jesus climb is a *theological* mountain. He is aligning his story with the story in Exodus 20, read in Jewish synagogues at Pentecost, and describing how Moses ascended Mount Sinai to receive the Law and deliver it to all Israel. His will be a *Christian* discourse for Pentecost.

For one of the first problems that Christian Jews will have faced was how the traditional Jewish festivals should be observed. They will obviously have wanted to retain the festivals with their traditional readings, but they will also have wanted to add a Christian dimension. Matthew had no problem with the Jewish Law itself. In his mind Jesus had not come to abolish, but to fulfil it (Matthew 5. 17-20). Even the least of the Law's demands must be observed. But this is not enough. Christian Jews must go beyond external observance and prove themselves far better men than the Scribes and Pharisees. They will observe the *spirit* of the Law and not just its letter. "You have learned that our forefathers were told 'Do not commit murder... But what I tell you is this...'" (Matthew 5.21). The formula is repeated a further five times in all – at Matthew 5.27, 5.31, 5.33, 5.38 and 5.43. It establishes the theme of this first section of the sermon. The Christian life involves going beyond. It demands the extraordinary.

To put the matter simply, therefore, the Sermon on the Mount is not a sermon that Jesus himself ever preached. It is a sermon for Christian Jews to be read at Pentecost, constructed by Matthew from the traditional Old Testament material and from the teaching of Jesus as he had received it in Mark's

Gospel. The inspiration of the sermon is Jesus', but the actual text is Matthew's. He is not a mindless editor, but a Christian Scribe, interpreting and expanding his material to produce perhaps the most memorable of all Christian discourses.

The Sermon on the Mount remains inspirational today but was the pre-eminent text of nineteenth century German liberalism and underlies Adolph Harnack's *What is Christianity?*[1], which was published in 1900 and sold a million copies. Harnack's book was a reaction against dogma and presented Christianity as a way of life. The Sermon also underlies Dietrich Bonhoeffer's *The Cost of Discipleship*[2], published in 1937 (their families were near-neighbours and Bonhoeffer, a generation younger than Harnack, was one of his students). For both, "Sermon on the Mount Christianity" represented the original, simple, radical Christian ideal, before it was corrupted and obscured by layer upon layer of dogma and doctrine.

A Rabbinic Discourse

But, for all its apparent simplicity, the Sermon on the Mount is an immaculately constructed discourse in the Rabbinic style and we owe its interpretation to Michael Goulder who, in his *Midrash and Lection in Matthew*[3], was the first person in modern times to discover its structure.

The Sermon begins with a series of eight Beatitudes, each beginning "How blessed are those who....". Series of Blessings and Cursings (Woes) were a traditional Jewish literary form and there are Old Testament examples in Deuteronomy 27 and 28. Matthew also has seven Woes in his discourse against the Scribes and Pharisees (Matthew 23) and Luke has four Blessings and four Woes at the beginning of his Sermon on the Plain (Luke 6. 20-26). Blessings promise good fortune and Woes dire punishments. But in Matthew's case his Beatitudes are also a summary of the sermon. The Christian life brings "blessings with persecutions". It demands everything of us, yet is infinitely rewarding.

So Matthew begins, in the Beatitudes, by summarising the challenges and the rewards – and then expounds them, but (in the Jewish style) does so from last to first, that is, backwards.

This explains the problem with Matthew 5.11: "How blessed *you are* when you suffer insults and persecution....". Some have taken this as a ninth beatitude, but it is in fact the beginning of the exposition of the eighth. It applies the eighth beatitude to those who are listening to the Sermon. For the Jewish style is always from last to first (from the back of a book to the front). So, too, with the genealogies in Genesis: "These are the descendants of the sons of Noah, Shem, Ham and Japheth. The sons of Japheth are..., the sons of Ham are..., the sons of Shem are..." (Genesis 10).

The Structure of the Sermon

This then is the structure of Matthew's discourse, with the individual Beatitudes expounded in reverse order:

(8) How blessed are the persecuted
> They will have a rich reward (5. 11-12)
> They are the salt of the earth (5.13)
> They are light for all the world (5. 14-16)
> An Interjection: The Jewish Law still stands, undiminished (5. 17-20)

(7) How blessed are the peacemakers
> Do not be angry, or abusive, or sneering (5. 21-22)
> Make peace with your brother (5. 23-24)
> Come to terms with your creditors (5. 25-26)

(6) How blessed are the pure in heart
> Do not lust (5. 27-30)
> Do not get divorced or marry a divorcee (5. 31-32)
> Do not swear an oath (5. 33-37)

(5) How blessed are the merciful
> Do not take revenge (5. 38-42)
> Love your enemies (5. 43-48)
> Do not parade your acts of charity (your mercies) (6. 1-4)

(4) How blessed are those who hunger and thirst for righteousness
> Do not parade your prayers (6. 5-8)
> The Lord's Prayer (6. 9-15)
> Do not parade your fasting (6. 16-18)

(3) How blessed are the gentle
    They will have treasure in heaven (6. 19-21)
    They have the generous eye (6. 22-24)
    They will be free of anxiety (6. 25-34)

(2) How blessed are the mourners (the penitent)
    Do not judge (7. 1-2)
    Do not reprove your brother (7. 3-5)
    Do not destroy other people's good name (7.6)

(1) How blessed are those who know that they are poor
    They ask, and seek, and knock (7. 7-11)

The summary of the Sermon (the kelal):
    Always treat others as you would like them to treat you
    (7.12)

The peroration (Be doers and not hearers only):
    Take the narrow and not the broad gate (7. 13-14)
    Follow the true prophets and not the false (7. 15-23)
    Build your house on rock and not on sand (7. 24-27)

A New Ten Commandments for Christians

The annual commemoration of the Jewish Festival of Pentecost, then, provided the occasion for the Sermon. Jewish Christians, for whom Matthew wrote, wanted to celebrate the Law Giving on Mount Sinai, but also its re-interpretation by Jesus. And Matthew turned here to Mark's story of Jesus' encounter with the young man of great wealth (Mark 10. 17-31). He is going to retain the story when he comes to it, but he also wants to use it now. Here, after all, is Jesus' interpretation of the Law, the very theme of his discourse.

Jesus begins his summary of the Law with the sixth commandment ("Do not murder") and proceeds from there - "Do not commit adultery" (the seventh commandment); "Do not steal" (the eighth); "Do not give false evidence" (the ninth); "Honour your father and mother" (traditionally the fifth); and "Love your neighbour as yourself" (a summary of our whole obligation to other people, replacing the tenth commandment). There are, obviously, complications here, which Michael Goulder addresses in his book, but it is sufficient for my purpose that this is Matthew's understanding of the second table of the Law (a careful comparison of the two texts, Mark's and Matthew's, shows that he has, in fact, glossed Mark's text). So these commandments provide his starting point in the first chapter of the Sermon. Matthew will expound the second table of the Law (our duty to other people) in the light of Jesus' teaching. It involves a radical re-interpretation since the original commandments are negative, whereas the "going beyond" will demand something positive and seemingly sacrificial.

To these six duties (Matthew 5. 21-48) Matthew adds three religious duties (Matthew 6. 1-18), albeit radically re-interpreted again (almsgiving, prayer and fasting). But that only makes nine duties, whereas we all know that there were *ten* commandments. And Matthew, too, can count, for he is urging his congregation, whom he hopes will feel that they "still fall short", "to go the whole way" (Matthew 19.21), as Jesus urged the rich young man to do. For this they must "sell their possessions" and "give to the poor" that they may have "riches in heaven". This provides Matthew with his tenth commandment – a man's decision to give away his wealth and possessions. He expounds it in the final paragraphs of Matthew 6. "Do not store up for yourselves treasure on earth" (6. 19-21). Have the generous eye (6. 22-23). Serve God rather than Money (6.24), and lead the carefree life of the birds and lilies (6. 25-34).

So Christian Jews, the members of Matthew's synagogue, keep the Jewish Law and honour it. But they also seek to live it out in the spirit of Jesus, radically. There are still ten commandments, but they have been re-interpreted – six duties to our neighbour, three duties to God, and (the real hallmark of a Christian ethic in Matthew's mind) a final, limitless commitment to a life of poverty in the service of other people.

The Sermon Re-interpreted

Many popular books have been written expounding the Sermon on the Mount, and the Beatitudes in particular, and in the light of our recent discovery of the Sermon's structure, have misunderstood and misinterpreted much of it. Some such books are still worth reading (Bonhoeffer's is), but Matthew's original meaning must still be preferred. There is no need to comment on every verse, but the clarification of the meaning of some individual verses and sections may be helpful.

So Matthew 5. 11-16 is indeed the beginning of the Sermon proper and expounds the last Beatitude ("How blessed are those who have suffered persecution for the cause of right"). But the sequence is interrupted at 5. 17-20, where Matthew sets out what he takes to be Jesus' attitude towards the Law. Pauline Christians took a very different view, but Matthew, a Jewish Christian, affirms the Jewish Law in every particular. Not even the least of its demands can be set aside. The problem with the Scribes and Pharisees, as Matthew makes plain in chapter 23, is not what they *say* but what they *do*. They sit in the chair of Moses and attention should be paid to their words. The problem is that they say one thing and do another (Matthew 23.3). They are hypocrites – they do not live by their own teaching. So Jesus, in Matthew's mind, did not set the Law aside. On the contrary those who keep it, as well as teach it, will stand high in the kingdom of heaven (Matthew 5.19).

The seventh Beatitude (Matthew 5.9) is the first of those which have been generally misunderstood. The peacemakers are not international statesmen who reconcile nations, but Christians who refuse to nurse anger against their brother (Matthew 5. 21-22), or bear grievances against him (Matthew 5. 23-24), but rather, instead, settle their debts (Matthew thinks of sins as debts), make peace and seek to be reconciled to him (Matthew 5. 25-26). Here, as elsewhere, it is clear that the Sermon on the Mount is addressed to men. And Matthew does not just state the case, but urges it. This is a sermon in the modern sense - it is direct and persuasive.

The sixth Beatitude, addressed to "those whose hearts are pure", is concerned with lust, adultery (its consequence, divorce), and truthfulness. But here Matthew has a problem, because Mark believed that Jesus was opposed to divorce in all circumstances (Mark 10. 1-12). Mark portrays the disciples as being surprised by this and so has Jesus repeat himself unambiguously. Matthew, however, knew that the Jewish Law allowed divorce on the grounds of adultery and cannot believe that Jesus can have meant what Mark records him as saying. So he glosses and introduces the famous Matthaean exception – "If a man divorces his wife *for any cause other than unchastity* he involves her in adultery." Notice again that Matthew is only concerned with what *men* may or may not do.

The fifth Beatitude ("How blessed are those who show mercy") asserts that the Christian is to eschew revenge, love his enemy, and do acts of charity (mercies) without ulterior motives. It is one of the most moving and compelling sections of the Sermon. There are no half measures in the Christian life and its extraordinary quality lies in its always wanting to do more than is asked for or expected.

The fourth Beatitude ("How blessed are those who hunger and thirst for righteousness") summarises the Christian's duty in relation to prayer and fasting. The Lord's Prayer is analysed in another section but it is worth noting that Matthew represents prayer as being the simplest of activities. There are no experts or beginners here. There is nothing to learn or be taught. No equipment is required – just openness and sincerity, and a desire to pray.

The third Beatitude ("How blessed are those of a gentle spirit") was probably suggested by Psalm 37 which contrasts the lot of a righteous and unrighteous man. The righteous man is patient (Psalm 37.7). "Day in, day out, he lends generously" (Psalm 37.26). And the Lord will reward him. "His inheritance shall last for ever. When times are bad, he shall not be distressed, and in days of famine he shall have enough" (Psalm 37. 18-19). So the Jewish Christian who follows Jesus' advice to the rich young man to "go the whole way, sell his possessions, and give to the poor" will find that God supplies all his needs so that he is enabled to live the carefree life of the birds and lilies.

The second Beatitude ("How blessed are the sorrowful", or "mourners") has again been misunderstood. These are not mourners in the usual sense of the word, nor are they sorrowful about any misfortune that has befallen them. They are sorrowful (they mourn) for their sins, and their reward is to find consolation (forgiveness). So they should not be judgemental, knowing that they themselves are under judgement (Matthew 7. 1-2). They should not find fault with their brother, knowing themselves to have greater faults (Matthew 7. 3-5). And they should not destroy other people's reputations, knowing that their own good name is unwarranted (Matthew 7.6).

Finally, the first Beatitude speaks of the blessedness of the poor, whose reward will be the kingdom of heaven. Their very poverty leads them to depend upon God. They ask and will receive (Matthew 7. 7-11).

So the Sermon is done and it only remains to sum up and exhort. Matthew 7.12 is intended as a summary of the whole sermon: "Always treat others as you would like them to treat you: that is the Law and the prophets".

But nothing can be left to chance. Too much is at stake. So the Sermon ends on a note of urgency. Blessings and Cursings (Woes) are a means of bringing people to a moment of decision. The Book of Deuteronomy as a whole is a book of sermons and, as Moses reminded Israel time and again but most movingly before his death, there is a choice to be made between "life and good, or death and evil" (Deuteronomy 30. 15-20), between obedience and disobedience. Each has their very different consequence. And so Matthew braces himself for his peroration. There is the narrow gate, or the broad way (Matthew 7. 13-14), the good tree or the poor tree (Matthew 7. 15-20). Talking is no good; it is doing that counts (Matthew 7. 21-24). And Matthew never over-elaborates. It is not a complicated decision we face, but a straightforward choice. We build our house on sand or rock, one or the other (Matthew 7. 24-27). It is as simple as that, and an awesome decision.

[1] *What is Christianity?* by Adolf Harnack is based on a series of open lectures that he gave in Berlin in the winter of 1899-1900. The first English translation was published by Williams and Norgate Ltd in 1901. A 5th edition was published by Ernest Benn Ltd in 1958.

[2] *The Cost of Discipleship* by Dietrich Bonhoeffer was first published in German in 1937, and in English in 1948 by the SCM Press.

[3] For a full and scholarly analysis of the Sermon, see chapters 12 – 14 of Michael Goulder's *Midrash and Lection in Matthew (SPCK 1974).*

THE PAULINE EPISTLES

PAUL IN HIS OWN WORDS

Paul was the dominant figure in the early church. A casual glance at the index to the New Testament will show that his Letters alone make up nearly a quarter of its total contents. By contrast, the Twelve, whom we might have expected to emerge as leaders, are mostly known to us only by name. They will have been Mark's principal historical source for the life of Jesus, but none of them wrote anything themselves that has survived (the five Letters attributed to Peter and John are not genuinely apostolic).

Of the thirteen Letters attributed to Paul, only the three so-called Pastoral Epistles (1 and 2 Timothy, and Titus) were definitely not written by him. They assume a settled church background and could date from as late as AD 110. The Letter to the Ephesians is also of doubtful authenticity, on account of its different style but, even if we exclude these four, we are still left with nine genuine Pauline Letters, all except the Letter to Philemon of some length. They were written between AD 45-60 and pre-date the Gospels. Their survival, through the willingness of disciples to copy, treasure and read them, is in itself testimony to Paul's unique authority.

The Acts of the Apostles is also a potential source for the life of Paul and indeed is very largely about him. Luke, its author, tells the story of Paul's conversion in chapter 9, and of his first missionary journey in chapters 13 and 14. Chapter 15 then describes how the Council of Jerusalem decided to waive the imposition of the Jewish Law on Paul's non-Jewish converts and so clear the way for his further ministry. Thereafter Acts is exclusively Paul's story - his ministry, trials, shipwreck, and arrival in Rome. There are no further references to Peter, or the Twelve, or the Deacons.

But there is a problem in evaluating the historical accuracy of Luke's story. It is clear, for example, that he decided to minimize the conflicts in the early church between Jewish and non-Jewish Christians, although they are very evident in Paul's Letters and were a continuing source of anxiety and frustration to him. Luke must also have felt that he knew much less about Paul than he would have wished. It is unlikely, for example, that he knew how Paul died. Some 200 years and more later Eusebius was to infer, in his History of the Church (Book 2, Chapter 22), that Paul had been martyred, relying on two verses from 2 Timothy 4. But they do not really support his inference and 2 Timothy, as we have seen, is not in any case a genuine Pauline epistle. In truth we do not know either how Paul died or what Luke's sources were in writing Acts. It is clear, however, that he felt as free to midrash as he had in his Gospel. But, while we can compare the Synoptic Gospels with one another and so see exactly what each is doing, we have no access to Luke's sources for Acts. It is the only one of its kind and we have nothing with which to compare it.

It is clear, however, that in the Acts of the Apostles, as in his Gospel, Luke had a theological purpose in mind. In his Gospel Luke's theme was discipleship and in the Acts of the Apostles he proposed to show how the life of the early church reflected the life of Jesus. In the story of the Twelve (Acts 1-5), Stephen and Philip (Acts 6-8), Peter (Acts 9-12) and Paul (Acts 13-28), the same cycle is repeated - the descent of the Spirit, a ministry, a death, and a resurrection. By contrast Paul's Letters lack this kind of sophistication. They are responses to real situations. He may only occasionally be autobiographical, but he is generally candid and we have no reason to disbelieve anything he tells us. There is a place for expounding and evaluating Luke's account of Paul's ministry, but there is a stronger case for treating Paul's own Letters as the primary source for his life and thought.

What Paul tells us about himself

Of Paul's Letters, the Letter to the Galatians is much the most autobiographical and revealing. Very briefly it tells us, first, that he had been a zealous Jew and, as such, had savagely persecuted the church (Galatians 1. 13-14). But then, God "chose to reveal his Son to me" and, when that happened, he went first to Arabia and only subsequently returned to Damascus, to which, like Luke, we may assume him to have been travelling (Galatians 1. 15-17). A few verses earlier he had referred to this experience as a "revelation of Jesus Christ" (Galatians 1.12) and it was the foundation of his apostleship and subsequent Christian ministry.

Paul first went to Jerusalem three years later and stayed a fortnight with Peter. There he also met James, the Lord's brother, but saw none of the other apostles (Galatians 1. 18-20). Then he went on to Syria and Cilicia (it would seem to begin his ministry) and did so without reference to the Judaean church, who only heard secondhand reports of what he was doing (Galatians 1. 21-24). Finally, fourteen years later still, he returned to Jerusalem again, with Barnabas and Titus, to report upon his mission and to seek the recognition and approval of the Jerusalem church for it (Galatians 2. 1-5). Agreement of a sort was reached but, as Paul makes absolutely clear, his relationship with Peter and the others was fraught and unhappy. He had a generally poor opinion of them.

If, therefore, we were to date Paul's conversion somewhat arbitrarily at AD c.35, his ministry would take us to AD c.55 at the very least. But this is speculation. Certainly Paul travelled very extensively, and over many years. He perhaps made three missionary journeys (we are dependent upon Luke for this), but any reading of his Letters will show that he rarely spent more than a year anywhere and had travelled throughout most of present-day Syria, Turkey and Greece. Of the churches to which he wrote, Corinth, Philippi and Thessalonica were in Greece, while Colosse, Ephesus and Galatia were in Turkey, although at the time all of these places were subject to the same Roman jurisdiction and were part of the Greek-speaking world. Paul may or may not have reached Rome (we only have Luke's word for this), but he certainly aspired to do so.

Several of the semi-autobiographical passages in Paul's Letters arise from his attempt to win the sympathy of his readers by contrasting their relative comfort, wealth, and ease, with the rigours and hardships of his own life. He therefore dramatizes, rather than makes light of them. So, in 1 Corinthians, he writes: "To this day we go hungry and thirsty and in rags; we are roughly handled; we wander from place to place; we wear ourselves out working with our own hands.

135

They curse us, and we bless; they persecute us, and we submit to it; they slander us, and we humbly make our appeal. We are treated like the scum of the earth, the dregs of humanity to this very day" (1 Corinthians 4. 11-13). Sometimes an element of "boasting" creeps in, as when he compares his sacrifices with those of other "sham-apostles". It is not clear who these are, but it is not a flattering way of referring to them. Of his own ordeals he writes: "Five times the Jews have given me thirty-nine strokes; three times I have been beaten with rods; once I was stoned; three times I have been shipwrecked, and for twenty-four hours I was adrift on the open sea. I have been constantly on the road; I have met dangers from rivers, dangers from foreigners, dangers from robbers, dangers in towns, dangers in the country, dangers at sea, dangers from false friends. I have toiled and I have drudged, I have often gone without sleep; hungry and thirsty, I have often gone fasting; and I have suffered from cold and exposure" (2 Corinthians 11. 24-27).

Paul does not explicitly mention imprisonment in this list of troubles, but he does in the Philippian Letter. He tells them, "When I lie in prison or appear in the dock to vouch for the truth of the Gospel, you all share in the privilege that is mine" (Philippians 1.7). It is a positive experience, for "my imprisonment in Christ's cause has become common knowledge to all at headquarters...and has given confidence to most of our fellow-Christians to speak the word of God fearlessly and with extraordinary courage" (Philippians 1. 13-14).

It is very unlikely that Paul was married. He reassures married people that it is quite allowable for them to have sex together (1 Corinthians 7. 1-7), but says this by way of concession, not command. "I should like you all to be as I am myself." And although Paul seems mostly not to have worked for his living, he asserts his right to do so if local churches were unwilling or unable to support him. "Have I no right to eat and drink? Have I no right to take a Christian wife about with me, like the rest of the apostles and the Lord's brothers, and Cephas? Or are Barnabas and I alone bound to work for our living?" (1 Corinthians 9. 5-6). But, he adds later, "I have availed myself of no such right." His only pay is "the satisfaction of preaching the Gospel without expense to anyone; in other words, of waiving the rights which my preaching gives me" (1 Corinthians 9.18). It therefore seems most likely, but not certain, that Paul was unmarried and that he worked intermittently. Some churches, it would seem, supported him, while others did not. Luke tells us that he was a tentmaker by trade (Acts 18.3), although the Letters provide no corroboration of this.

Paul, an Apostle of Christ Jesus by God's Call

It may not at first sight seem a contentious thing for Paul to begin five of his nine Letters with such words as these, but it was very deliberately done and was a claim that some resisted. In Galatians Paul is even more explicit: "From Paul, an apostle, *not by human appointment or human commission*, but by commission from Jesus Christ and from God the Father who raised him from the dead" (Galatians 1.1). Who, then, were the humans, whose appointment and commissioning might have been thought necessary? They were Peter, and the Twelve, and James the Lord's brother. Paul is insisting that he is quite their equal and owes nothing to them. It is Jesus himself who appointed him an apostle. His authority and legitimacy is independent of theirs.

Three groups, here, need to be distinguished - the Twelve, disciples, and apostles. The Twelve are listed in each of the three Synoptic Gospels, although the lists are not quite identical. So we more or less know their names, but little more (Mark 3. 13-19; Matthew 10. 2-4; Luke 6. 12-16). Twelve was a significant number because Jacob's twelve sons gave their names to the Twelve Tribes of Israel and, if the church were to be thought of as the New Israel, there would be symbolical significance in it, too, having twelve founders. Mark writes of the Twelve more commonly than the other evangelists, but they all use the title at least once. The names of the other two groups are explained by their derivation. A disciple is one who learns and an apostle is one who is sent. The names seem in places to be interchangeable, but apostles were effectively an elite group, chosen from a much larger number of disciples. Luke uses the title "apostle" in his Gospel more commonly than Matthew and Mark, who use it only once, and it becomes his usual way of referring to the Twelve in the Acts of the Apostles. But Luke also regarded Barnabas and Paul as apostles, and Paul refers to Andronicus and Junias as apostles in his commendations at the end of the Letter to the Romans (Romans 16.7).

The question of Paul's apostleship is the dominant issue in the two Corinthian Letters and in the Letter to the Galatians, where Paul describes his three meetings with Peter. Short of going through all three Letters in detail, it is easiest to begin at 1 Corinthians 9. 1-2: "Am I not a free man? Am I not an apostle? Did I not see Jesus our Lord? Are not you my own handiwork, in the Lord? *If others do not accept me as an apostle,* you at least are bound to do so, for you are yourselves the very seal of my apostolate, in the Lord." Paul seems to accept that he is not an apostle in quite the same way that the Twelve are, but bases his claim, which he regards as indisputable, upon three criteria.

First, and most importantly, Paul has himself, like the Twelve, "seen the Lord". He is referring to the revelation that he received when he became a Christian and which he counts as a post-resurrection appearance. He lists it as such in 1 Corinthians 15. 8-11: "In the end he appeared even to me; though this birth of mine was monstrous, for I had persecuted the church and am therefore inferior to all other apostles - indeed not fit to be called an apostle. However, I am what I am [that is, an apostle], nor has his grace been given to me in vain. On the contrary, in my labours I have outdone them all [that is, the other apostles]...". In the Galatian Letter, as well, he explicitly emphasises that none of the other apostles had anything to do with his commission. They had no part in it: "When that happened [referring to his revelation], *without* consulting any human being, *without* going up to Jerusalem to see those who were apostles before me, I went off at once to Arabia, and afterwards returned to Damascus" (Galatians 1. 15-17). He cannot make himself any clearer - his apostleship was God's doing.

Secondly, as Paul implies in the first of these quotations, he has been the most successful of all the apostles in founding churches. The proof of his divine commission is the success that

138

has attended his ministry. And thirdly, no lesser people than James, the Lord's brother, Peter and John have openly accepted him as an apostle (Galatians 2. 9-10). So why do others dispute it? Paul almost despairs at having continually to set out his credentials and argue with his detractors.

The Jewish - Gentile Conflict

Luke's first descriptions of the early church portray its life and fellowship as idyllic (Acts 3. 42-47). But in Acts 15 he refers for the first time to a "fierce dissension and controversy" that arose over the necessity, or not, of requiring non-Jewish Christians to be circumcised (Acts 15. 1-2). A meeting is arranged (the so-called Council of Jerusalem, referred to above) to which Paul and Barnabas are welcomed. A decision is taken by the apostles and elders, with Peter and James, the Lord's brother, as their spokesman, and it is that the requirements of the Law need not be enforced. Letters to this effect are drawn up and ordered to be read in the Gentile churches. So the dispute is happily resolved and the consideration which weighed most heavily with the apostles in reaching their decision was that God had already shown his favour towards the Gentile converts by bestowing the Holy Spirit upon them.

It would seem, however, that the matter was not as easily resolved as Luke suggests and indeed may never have been resolved. It is most likely that the Jewish and Gentile churches just went their own ways. The Pauline Gentile churches grew and spread, while the Jewish churches remained in Judaea and over two or three centuries dwindled and eventually disappeared. They came to be known as Ebionites (Hebrew for the "poor ones") and Eusebius mistakenly thought of them as heretics (Book III, chapter 27). Some denied the Virgin Birth, and all thought of Jesus as "a man plain and ordinary". They observed the Jewish Sabbath and the Jewish Law, read Matthew's Gospel and rejected the Pauline Epistles. Their name probably indicated that they led lives of poverty (Jesus had enjoined this) and Eusebius concedes that they also met on Sunday to celebrate the resurrection of Jesus. But he had no time for them.

The principal Jewish practices to which Paul objected were the keeping of the Jewish calendar, the practice of circumcision, and the rules governing kosher food. So Paul charges the Galatian church: "You keep special days and months and seasons and years" (Galatians 4.10). He had here the Jewish calendar in mind, which revolved around lunar months and pilgrim festivals (Pesah, Shabuoth and Sukkoth, to give them their Jewish names) and for which Matthew's Gospel provided special readings. Paul also thought the practice of circumcision particularly divisive and unnecessary. There are, amazingly, more passages referring to circumcision in Paul's Letters than in the whole of the Old Testament and it indicates that circumcision came to represent the *whole* practice of Judaism, which Paul wished to shed. Less important but also an issue, were the rules governing kosher food. Paul very openly criticises Cephas (Peter), when he backtracks and gives in to conservative Jews over this matter (Galatians 2. 11-14). And the disputes and divisions to which he often refers (for example, in Romans 16. 17-20) almost certainly arise through attempts by Jewish Christians to force Jewish practices on Paul's non-Jewish converts.

With the wisdom of hindsight it is easy to see the force of Paul's arguments. Jesus himself and all his first disciples may have been practising Jews, but if Christianity were ever to become a world religion it was essential, at the very least, that it asserted its independence of Judaism and its distinctively Jewish culture.

What Paul Knew and Believed

It is interesting to ask, next, what Paul knew about Jesus. He had, of course, never met Jesus himself, although he thought of his "revelation" as some kind of personal encounter with him.

Paul certainly knew the tradition of the Last Supper. At 1 Corinthians 11. 17-34 he berates the Corinthian church for the disorder that results when they "meet as a congregation", and then goes on to describe the institution of the Last Supper. As elsewhere he stresses that what he knows of this tradition "came to me from the Lord himself" and again not, we therefore infer, from the disciples. This is almost as full an account as is found in the Synoptic Gospels, and Luke, indeed, prefers to follow Paul's version of the bread and cup words. But Paul omits to say that the Last Supper was a Passover Meal (if it was) or to make any reference to Judas' betrayal. We can infer that commemorations of the Last Supper were a feature of church life in Corinth and that Paul was well aware of the tradition.

Paul obviously also knew that Jesus died by crucifixion, although he never alludes to the circumstances surrounding his death. He refers to the "cross of Christ" and to "Christ crucified" many, many times, and crucifixion becomes a metaphor for the Christian life. We must be crucified with Christ, as Paul believed he had been. But he never explains that Jesus died by judicial execution at the hands of the Roman authorities, or hints at the charges which he faced. For Paul it was almost as if Jesus' death was a theological death - "he died for our sins, in accordance with the Scriptures" (1 Corinthians 15.2).

Paul also knew the tradition regarding Jesus' resurrection: "He was raised to life on the third day, according to the Scriptures" and appeared to a succession of people. In fact Paul is more specific than the Gospels with regard to the resurrection appearances. "He appeared to Cephas, and afterwards to the Twelve. Then he appeared to over 500 of our brethren at once, most of whom are still alive, though some have died. Then he appeared to James [the Lord's brother?], and afterwards to all the apostles" (1 Corinthians 15. 5-7). But Paul does not refer to the tradition of the Empty Tomb. Again, for him, the resurrection is almost a theological event and resurrection is as much a metaphor for the Christian life as crucifixion.

At this point the different perspectives of Jewish and Pauline Christianity emerge. Mark and Matthew represent Jewish Christianity and their perspective sets the story of the life of Jesus within an eschatological framework. Eschatology (from the Greek word, *eschatos*, meaning "last") is the study of the process by which the End of the World will come. Mark and Matthew thought that the coming of Jesus had brought that End very near, but that the kingdom of God would only be finally realised with the Return, or *Second* Coming, of Jesus at Passover.

Paul's, and Luke's, perspective was slightly different. They were charismatics, who believed that the proof of God's endorsement of Paul's Gentile ministry was to be found in the signs and miracles that attended it (Acts 15. 6-12). So Luke was to describe the outpouring of God's Spirit at Pentecost and, in the Acts of the Apostles, provide a foundation document which integrated the Pauline churches within the overall scheme of things and awarded them an equal place with Jewish Christians in the church.

The Pauline Gospel

Paul, too, expected the Return of Jesus within his lifetime but, in his view, Christians did not need to know (and certainly might not know) anything about Jesus' life or teaching. For Paul, Christianity was a Gospel of salvation, one that he had experienced himself and wished others to share. There was no narrative to it. Pauline Christianity was primarily theological.

The biggest issue of all was Jesus himself. This subject is known today as Christology and the debate continued, long after Paul's death, into the middle of the fifth century, when the doctrine of the Person of Christ was finally defined (although not to everyone's satisfaction) at the Council of Chalcedon. Essentially the question is whether Jesus was or was not God, pure and simple, a divine figure, and if he was God, as the church came to believe, how his divinity could be reconciled with his humanity.

As part of this continuing debate New Testament scholars today often discuss the Christology of the Synoptic Gospels. What did Mark, Matthew and Luke believe about Jesus? Can they be accommodated within Pauline, and subsequent Christian, orthodoxy? The truthful answer is "only with great difficulty, if at all". As we have seen, Eusebius condemned Jewish Christians for believing that Jesus was "a man plain and ordinary". He does not do justice to them, but he is right in saying that they did not think of Jesus as divine. For them he was the Messiah or Christ (these are alternative Hebrew and Greek titles), the Son of God (but not in a literal sense), and the Son of Man. Each of these titles has its own derivation and history, but none of them imply pre-existence or divinity.

Paul's precise views are not entirely clear, but he certainly thought of Jesus as all but divine. He never actually says that Jesus *is* God, but he comes close to doing so. The relevant texts are often quoted. Paul writes in the Letter to the Colossians, for example, "He is the image of the invisible God; his is the primacy over all created things. In him everything in heaven and on earth was created.... the whole universe has been created through him and for him. And he exists before everything, and all things are held together in him". For in him "the complete being of God, by God's own choice, came to dwell" (Colossians 1. 15-19). This paragraph can be read in conjunction with Philippians 2. 5-11: "For the divine nature was his from the first... Bearing the human likeness, revealed in human shape, he humbled himself, and in obedience accepted even death - death on a cross." At the very least Paul believed in the pre-existence of Jesus, and John's Gospel, whether faithfully or not, represented the Pauline Jesus to a later generation. For John, Jesus is the Word of God in human flesh, who speaks of himself in divine terms, has foreknowledge of future events, and only eats to keep up the appearance of being human.

Paul's Letter to the Romans stands first in the Pauline canon and is the only letter to expound Paul's theology systematically. A significant proportion of those to whom he was writing would seem to have been Jewish Christians but, whether they were Jewish or Gentile, Paul argues that *all* have sinned and stand in need of God's forgiveness. Abraham, who pre-dated Moses and the Law, can be thought of as a common ancestor to both and his faith in God is the faith to which both Jewish and Gentile Christians should aspire. But, of course, our common ancestry goes back even further than that - to Adam. And as Adam was the cause of our downfall, Jesus can be thought of as a Second Adam and the cause of our salvation. His death has made salvation possible. "Christ died for us [the wicked], while we were yet sinners, and that is God's proof of his love towards us. And so, since we have now been saved by Christ's sacrificial death, we shall all the more certainly be saved through him from final retribution" (Romans 5. 6-9).

As, therefore, Paul had begun a debate in the Letters to the Philippians and Colossians as to the exact status of Jesus (whether he is God or not), in the Letter to the Romans he discusses salvation. This later came to be known as the Atonement - how sinners are reconciled to God and what Jesus' role was in effecting that reconciliation. A crucial passage is found earlier at Romans 3. 23-26. Paul writes: "God designed Jesus to be the means of expiating sin by his sacrificial death, effective through faith." Does Paul mean that Jesus' death is to be thought of as a literal sacrifice, in the sense that, by dying, he has volunteered to be *punished* by God *instead* of us? Or was Paul just writing metaphorically? Again there is no way of knowing certainly, but he appears to be inclining towards the first of these views.

As we come to the end of this chapter some readers may feel that it has all been rather heavy going. But Paul's Letters themselves are not an easy read. Most congregations at the Eucharist prefer the Gospel to the Epistle. Paul deals in theology rather than narrative, doctrines rather than stories. His Letters are certainly intense - his was not a sheltered life and many passages are very moving. But Paul was also quite confrontational and combative - he was a controversial person and uncompromising in his views. The Letters are also *working* documents, responses to particular situations and inevitably leave many subjects unaddressed. On many occasions we would like to know more. But above all Paul's Letters are a testimony to the loyalty which he inspired. He was, in his own words, the "Apostle to the Gentiles" (Galatians 2. 6-8) and the church's growth beyond the narrow confines of Judaism would seem to have been largely attributable to him.

THE NEW TESTAMENT IN USE

BIBLICAL MANUSCRIPTS, THEIR TRANSLATION AND THE INVENTION OF PRINTING

When people read the Bible or hear it read in church, they may sometimes wonder where it all comes from. They are hearing it read in translation, of course, but who translated it and what exactly were they translating?

The individual books of the New Testament were written, in Greek, between 1,900 and 1,950 years ago. So the autograph manuscripts have not survived. We do not have the very pieces of papyrus or vellum that Mark, Matthew, Luke, John or Paul wrote on. In fact we do not have the autograph manuscript of any book written so long ago. All books from the ancient world only survive because someone else, and usually many people, have made copies of them.

Papyrus only survives in a dry climate and is very brittle and easily damaged. So there is no complete early papyrus manuscript of the New Testament. The finest is the Chester Beattie papyrus (named after the man who acquired it in 1931), which was found in Egypt near Hermopolis. It was originally a complete Bible, but very little of the Gospels has survived, so the manuscript is really only valuable in determining variant readings in the chapters that it covers. Nevertheless papyrus manuscripts are generally older than vellum and the Chester Beattie papyrus is said to date from the third century.

Vellum (parchment), made from the skin of sheep or goats, was obviously very much more expensive than papyrus and all surviving vellum manuscripts date from the fourth century or later. Successive persecutions of the church obviously took their toll of Bibles, which were commonly burnt. It will have been very disheartening for persecuted congregations to see the labour of many hours destroyed and their churches left without any Bible at all. But following the Edict of Milan in 313, the Emperor Constantine tried to make restitution and the commissioning of new copies of the Bible almost certainly dates from this period. Even so, only five vellum manuscripts from the fourth and fifth centuries survive and two of these have many gaps.

All modern Greek New Testaments begin by listing these manuscripts, both vellum and papyrus, in a Critical Apparatus and each manuscript is assigned a number or letter. The Chester Beattie papyrus, for example, is p45. The core vellum manuscripts are Sinaiticus (denoted by the Hebrew letter Aleph where possible, or S where not), Alexandrinus (A), and Vaticanus (B). All of these are codices (pages rather than scrolls) and so Sinaiticus is correctly called the Codex Sinaiticus. It has four columns per page, where Alexandrinus has two. They are written in Uncial Script (that is, in capital letters) with no gaps between words. Words also run over from one line to another and there are elisions. So, in Sinaiticus, "Jesus" is shortened to IC (IS in Roman script). There are also spelling mistakes and corrections. The early history of these manuscripts is not known, but Alexandrinus was presented to the Patriarch of Alexandria in 1098 and given by one of his successors to Charles I. Sinaiticus was found as recently as 1849 by a German scholar, Constantine Tischendorf, in St Catherine's Monastery in Sinai. It came by a circuitous and devious route into the hands of the Russian Government and was sold to the British Museum in 1933 for £100,000. The Codex Vaticanus is in the Vatican Library and is not, to the best of my knowledge, on display, but both Alexandrinus and Sinaiticus can be seen in the new British Library building in London[1]. Sinaiticus is interesting in including the Shepherd of Hermas and the Letter of Barnabas, which are not now regarded as belonging to the New Testament. There is a copy of the facsimile edition of Sinaiticus in Dr Williams' Library[2].

The New Testament, then, was written in Greek, the language of the Eastern Roman Empire. The Western Church, however, spoke Latin and it was Jerome (342-420) who translated the Bible, from the Hebrew and Greek, into Latin. His was not the first such translation, but it became the standard one and is known today as the Vulgate (the Editio Vulgata, the common or generally used edition). Jerome was the outstanding scholar of his generation and was later regarded (with Gregory, Ambrose, and Augustine) as one of the four Doctors of the Church. His translation was used, unchallenged, throughout Western Europe for more than 1,000 years. His *is* the Latin Bible. The Codex Bezae (named after Theodore Beza, who gave it to Cambridge University) is a fifth or sixth century manuscript (denoted by the letter D) which has both the Greek and Latin texts, the Greek on the left hand page and Jerome's Latin translation on the right. It is not complete, however, and is not nearly as beautifully written as Sinaiticus. Huge numbers of hand-written copies of the Vulgate survive.

Wycliffite Bibles

In the late fifteenth and early sixteenth centuries two important developments occurred which were to have immense repercussions. The first chronologically, but only by a few years, was the translation of the New Testament into English (and indeed into other European languages as well). The second was the invention of printing.

The first English translation of the Bible (from the Vulgate, not from the Greek) was for many years attributed to John Wyclif, whose followers were known as Lollards. But it was almost certainly the work of Nicholas of Hereford and John Purvey, who made their translation with his encouragement, and perhaps help. Wyclif died in 1384. Latin was still the language of scholarship and the law (French was the language of the Court), but ordinary people spoke English. Wyclif believed that everyone should have access to the Bible and as many as 250 Lollard Bibles have survived. They are, of course, all hand written, some beautifully so, and were presumably the possession of wealthy people. The translations are not uniform and there is little or nothing to identify them as specifically Wycliffite Bibles. Even those with glosses betray no partisan commitment. Unauthorized ownership of them was not dangerous until after 1409. The present authority on the Lollards is Anne Hudson, whose *The Premature Reformation*[3] tells their story in fascinating detail.

The Gutenberg Bible and Invention of Printing

The great spur to translation, however, was the discovery of "the art of multiplying books", as it was called at the time, and the very first book to be printed with movable metal type was the Gutenberg Bible, which was printed in 1455. It was enormously expensive to produce. Johannes Gutenberg, who lived in Mainz, borrowed some 1,600 guilders from his partner, Johann Fust, to buy or make the press and the typeface with which it was printed, at a time when a decent town house would cost less than 100 guilders. Sadly it led to his bankruptcy, but the Bible itself was a quite magnificent achievement. Between 150 and 200 copies were printed, some on vellum and some on paper, and of these 48 survive, about 20 of them complete. The British Library in London has several copies and one is almost always on display. They also have a small, nicely illustrated history of the Gutenberg Bible by Martin Davies[4] on sale at their bookstall.

Gutenberg's Bible has forty-two lines of type with two columns per page and is also known as the forty-two line Bible. The type-face mimics handwriting so that, from a distance, the book appears to be handwritten, with only capital letters left out for manual rubrication. In this way individual copies could be decorated with whatever elaboration was judged appropriate. It is thought that they originally sold for twenty guilders so that they were effectively cheap, imitation copies of handwritten manuscripts, although we will see them today as beautiful examples of the new art of printing. Each book of the Bible is prefaced with Jerome's Prologue and a space, six lines deep and half a column across, is left for whatever illustration is chosen. The Book of Proverbs in one British Library paper copy has a splendid picture of Solomon, and the margins of the page are decorated with wildlife miniatures. For, as we know, Solomon "discoursed of trees, from the cedars of Lebanon down to the marjoram that grows out of the wall, of beasts and birds, of reptiles and fishes" (1 Kings 4. 31-34). This was an illuminator's opportunity! A space is also left at the very beginning for the title of the book to be added in red ink, and the capital letters at the beginning of each sentence also have a small red infilling. As an economy the typeface was broken up and reused as each section was printed, producing what was, effectively, a limited edition. Maybe, one day, an affordable facsimile will be published.

The art of printing spread very quickly and particularly on mainland Europe. The typefaces and presses were not in themselves expensive and the only constraint was the high cost of rag paper. By the 1520s Cologne, Antwerp, Bruges and Paris had all become centres of book production - London lagged behind, largely on account of censorship. William Caxton was the first to set up a press in England, but all his books were on secular subjects (chess, philosophy, history). Even had he wished to do so, it would have been quite impossible for him to print a copy of the Bible in English.

The Reformation and First Vernacular Translations

Although there were several false beginnings (the Lollards in England, the Hussites in Bohemia) the Reformation can best be dated as beginning in 1520. This was the year in which Martin Luther published his three famous Manifestos - to the Nobility of the German Nation respecting the Reformation of the Christian Estate, On the Babylonish Captivity of the Church, and Concerning Christian Liberty. Thousands of copies of these and other Lutheran tracts and sermons were printed and sufficient numbers reached England for at least two good bonfires. One of these, held in 1521 outside St Paul's Cathedral in London, was presided over by Cardinal Wolsey. Brian Moynahan, in his biography of William Tyndale[5], has an amusing account of the many ways in which first tracts, and later Bibles, were smuggled into England. Without printing the Reformation could never have become a popular movement.

After his condemnation and excommunication by Pope Leo X in 1521, Luther and his supporters were at great risk and Frederick the Wise, the Elector of Saxony, a long-time supporter of Luther's, arranged for him to be "kidnapped" on his way back from the Diet of Worms and "imprisoned" (given sanctuary) in the Wartburg Castle at Eisenach. Here Luther began, and perhaps finished, his historic translation of the New Testament into everyday German from Jerome's Latin text. The first edition ran to 4,000 copies and so quickly sold out that entreprising printers soon began to run off pirate editions. Within four years it had been reprinted fourteen times in Wittenberg alone. The Old Testament followed shortly afterwards.

Martin Luther's translation of the Bible into German was William Tyndale's inspiration for undertaking his own first printed translation of the Bible into English, except that he worked, not from the Latin text as Luther had done, but from the original Greek and Hebrew. Tyndale studies have experienced a recent very welcome revival with David Daniell's splendid biography[6], but Tyndale's early life in this country is not inherently interesting and from 1524 onwards, when he left for the continent, it was inevitably shrouded in secrecy. He settled first in Cologne, but was then forced to move to Worms, where he may have been helped with his Hebrew by the Jewish community there. The Cologne New Testament was to have been printed on quarto sheets (very roughly nine inches by twelve inches) and some pages of Matthew's Gospel survive in this format. But in Worms he abandoned this edition and his famous 1526 New Testament was printed octavo (eight pages to the sheet of paper), very roughly paper-back size. This both saved on the cost of paper and made them much easier to smuggle back to England. Until very recently only one complete copy was thought to have survived, albeit missing its title page, and this is on view at the British Library in London. But in 1996 another absolutely complete copy, with its title page, was found in a library in Germany.

Parts of the Old Testament were translated and published in the following years (the Pentateuch, first of all), but instead of completing this project Tyndale returned to the New Testament and in 1534 published a revised translation, with biblical cross references, prologues before each book, woodcut illustrations, and a title page acknowledging Tyndale himself as the translator. Copies were six inches tall, four inches wide, and one and a half inches thick. It was printed in Antwerp. But sadly, in 1535, Tyndale was betrayed, arrested, and in August 1536 was condemned for heresy. He was then strangled and burnt at the stake. John Foxe, in his *Acts and Monuments*, is our principal source for this[7].

The Authorised and Revised Versions

Miles Coverdale's English Bible was the next to appear, in 1535, and on this occasion at the request of Convocation and with the tacit agreement of the Henry VIII, to whom it was dedicated. But this, and successive other English translations, were all deeply indebted to Tyndale's and were often revisions of his. Coverdale's only lasting contribution to translation rests in his Psalter, which has survived in the Church of England's Book of Common Prayer.

Other translations followed – the Great Bible in 1539, the Geneva (or Breeches) Bible in 1557, and the Bishops' Bible in 1568. These last two, for the first time, divided the text into verses. But the Authorized Version of the Bible (the so-called A.V. or King James Bible), which dates from 1611, is much the best known of the sixteenth and seventeenth century translations today. The title page reads, "The Holy Bible containing the Old and New Testaments translated out of the original tongues and with the former translations diligently compared and revised by His Majesty's special command. Appointed to be read in church." The words "Authorized Version" do not appear and are simply our name for it. The "original tongues" are Hebrew and Greek (Latin was not an original tongue); "the former translations" include the Great, Geneva and Bishops' Bible, but most particularly Tyndale's 1534 New Testament; and "his Majesty" is King James I. The decision to proceed with this new translation was taken at the Hampton Court Conference in 1604 and some 50 scholars are said to have been involved. Today the Authorized Version is always printed with modern spelling, which is a pity in some ways since its early seventeenth English would show that it was some 400 years old. But, for all that so many scholars were involved, the Authorized Version is not a new translation but a revision, and a revision primarily of Tyndale's magnificent 1534 translation.

The Authorized Version remains, for some people, *the* English Bible to this day and is still the preferred translation in many churches. But a Revised Version was published in 1881 (the so-called R.V.) to take account of contemporary research and recently discovered manuscripts. It was a work of patient scholarship and as late as the 1960s was the preferred translation for examination purposes in the Oxford University Theology School.

Modern English Translations

J.B.Phillips, by chance once a curate of the church of which I became Rector, had great success in the immediate post war years with his *Letters to Young Churches* (the New Testament Epistles) and with his translation of the Gospels, but a flood of New Translations was about to appear, all of them the outcome of collaboration and targeted at specific constituencies within the Church. So, today, anyone walking into a bookshop and wanting a Bible is faced, not only with an array of different translations, but with different editions of each of them. Like the continental printers of the 1520s, today's publishers seem to have found the Bible a very profitable book!

Broadly there are five modern alternatives – the American Standard Version of 1907 with its updates (the Revised Standard Version of 1946 and the New Revised Standard Version of 1995), the New English Bible of 1961 (and its update, the Revised English Bible of 1989), the Jerusalem Bible of 1966 (and its update, the New Jerusalem Bible of 1985), the Good News Bible of 1976, and the New International Version (N.I.V) of 1978. All of these have merits and for practical use are probably preferable to the Authorised Version, which, of course, is still available and will always be treasured. Most people are likely to remain loyal to the translation that they grew up with (the New English Bible in my own case), but new readers will probably buy the most recent revision of the translation they choose.

The Revised Standard Version is the product of American scholarship but is available in both an American English and Anglicised version. It is more widely read in the United States than in England but is a worthy translation.

The New English Bible (a British translation) broke new ground when it was first published in several respects. It did not look like a Bible, but like a secular book, with a traditional dust jacket. It had no gilt-edged pages or wrap-around leather cover. The text was not divided into verses, but set out in paragraphs, again like secular books. And the books themselves were not attributed to *St* Matthew or *St* Mark, but simply to Matthew and Mark, as in the original manuscripts. It is more given to paraphrase than many would wish, but uses the best modern English idioms and a wide vocabulary.

The Jerusalem Bible is the translation for Roman Catholics, has the Nihil Obstat, and is published by a traditional Catholic publisher (Darton, Longman and Todd). It betrays very little bias and is also highly regarded.

The New International Version is for conservative evangelicals and its translators, in the words of the Preface, were "united in their commitment to the authority and infallibility of the Bible as God's Word in written form".

The Good News Bible (published by Hodder and Stoughton, a traditional evangelical publisher) uses the simplest English of all the modern translations and is widely used in schools. It has the smallest vocabulary. So Herod, on hearing of a child born to be king of the Jews, was "very upset" in the Good News Bible, "greatly perturbed" in the New English Bible, "troubled" in the Authorised Version, and "very frightened" in one of the other modern translations. "Very upset" (like Mummy, when something goes wrong) is obviously unsatisfactory, but try explaining what "greatly perturbed" means to an eight-year-old child, whom you are coaching for a Christmas Carol Service! Most translations have some merit and in general the standard of translation is very high.

[1] The British Library, 96 Euston Road, London NW1 (020 7412 7332 for Visitor Information) has both the Codex Sinaiticus and Codex Alexandrinus on permanent display.

[2] Dr Williams' Library, 14 Gordon Square, London WC1 (020 7387 3727) is a wonderful theological library and is open to the general public. It has facsimile copies (now sadly out of print) of both the Codex Sinaiticus and the Codex Bezae.

[3] *The Premature Reformation, Wycliffite texts and Lollard History*, by Anne Hudson (Clarendon Press, Oxford 1988).

[4] The *Gutenberg Bible* by Martin Davies (The British Library 1996).

[5] *If God Spare My Life* by Brian Moynahan (Little, Brown 2002).

[6] *William Tyndale, A biography* by David Daniell (Yale University Press 1994). He has also edited Tyndale's 1534 translation with modern spelling (Yale University Press 1989), and written *Let there be Light - William Tyndale and the making of the English Bible* (British Library 1994).

[7] *Acts and Monuments* by John Foxe 1563 is a very long book and almost certainly out of print, but a nineteenth-century edition can be seen in Dr Williams' Library.

THE CHRISTIAN LECTIONARY[1]

Anyone writing a book does so with an intention. It is a big commitment and would be a pointless exercise unless there were some end in view. We may therefore ask what intention inspired the writing of the individual books of the New Testament. What did Mark, Matthew, Luke and John have in mind when they put pen to papyrus? And what did they do with their manuscripts when they had finished them? Their Gospels could have been personal memoirs, left in a drawer as a record of the life of Jesus for posterity. But the problem with this is that most things are done to meet an *immediate* need and, unless the evangelists had a practical end in view, no one would have copied their manuscripts to ensure their survival.

Paul's Letters, certainly, could have been letters in the modern sense. They address present problems and disputes, and end with personal greetings. But, perhaps, they were not just read privately by a few, but in church before a whole congregation. And, maybe, the longer letters at the very least were read on successive Sundays in a series of instalments. Other people might then have asked whether *they* could have a copy to read in *their* church. So copies of Paul's Letters would proliferate and be collected. They would have been a permanent resource in Pauline churches, so that some part of one of his letters might be read most Sundays, or even *every* Sunday. Effectively Paul's Letters would then have become Scripture.

Might, then, the Synoptic Gospels also have been written to meet a similar need in both Jewish and Pauline Christian churches? They might not have been written all at once, like individual Pauline Letters, but on a weekly basis to provide a Christian input into a synagogue service. Mark might then have accumulated modules (*pericope*) and perhaps reused them another year when the same Torah reading would recur. So his Gospel would have been put together, story by story, to meet a *present* need. And then, as happened with Paul's Letters, individual synagogues might ask for a copy of Mark's material, so that they could use it as well. And so, again, copies would

155

proliferate. Single copies of a book stood little chance of survival in the ancient world, especially when written on papyrus.

These might not seem unreasonable suggestions, but they have not been well received. This chapter cannot hope to convince the academic sceptic, who is referred to the books listed in the first footnote, but there is scope to explain and illustrate the theory to others.

The Jewish Calendar

With the earth going round the sun once every 365.26 days and the interval between successive news moons being 29.53 days, all calendars are complicated. The Jewish Calendar is based upon twelve lunar months of twenty-nine or thirty days, with an extra month in seven years out of nineteen. These months are Nisan (March-April), Iyyar, Sivan, Tammuz, Ab, Elul, Tishri (roughly, our October), Cheshvan, Kislev (December), Tebeth, Shebat, Adar, and (the extra month when required) Second Adar. Days run from sundown, rather than midnight.

Today there are eight major Jewish festivals and fasts, each with their own themes and readings. The most important of these in the New Testament period were Passover, Pentecost, New Year, the Day of Atonement, Tabernacles and Hanukkah. So, if the Synoptic Gospels followed this annual pattern of commemoration, we should expect them to have provided appropriate Christian readings. A table at the end of the chapter lists these festivals, with their themes and lections.

On Sabbaths not falling within these festivals, there would be a series of consecutive *weekly* readings. The most important of these are the fifty-four Torah[2] readings from Genesis, Exodus, Leviticus, Numbers and Deuteronomy. Typically two or three chapters are read each week and might take between fifteen and twenty minutes to read. Each reading has a name, much as the Psalms and Canticles in the Christian tradition are commonly known by their first one or two words (Psalm 95 is the *Venite*, the Song of Simeon the *Nunc Dimittis*). So, to quote the names of one or two Torah readings at random, the first is called *In the Beginning*, the eighth *And he sent*, the seventeenth *Jethro*, and the

54th *This is the blessing*. These fifty-four readings continue in use in Jewish synagogues today.

There then followed a much shorter reading from one of the five cycles of prophetic writings - either from the Former Prophets (Joshua, Judges, 1 and 2 Samuel and 1 and 2 Kings), or Isaiah, or Jeremiah, or Ezekiel, or from the Minor Prophets (the Twelve). This second reading was known as the Haphtarah (Hebrew for "the closer"). Jewish synagogues in the first century AD, therefore, had two cycles of Sabbath readings, the Torah and the Haphtarah, and these will have been the readings which the first Christian Jewish synagogues used and knew.

But, with time, things were further complicated by the addition of a third reading from the Writings[3], or Wisdom Literature (Job, Proverbs or Ecclesiasticus), and by the corruption of Hebrew into Aramaic. So, when Hebrew was no longer understood, a Targum, or translation-cum-commentary, followed the Torah and Haphtarah reading, effectively doubling the time that they took to read.

The Reading of Scripture in the Early Church

Before we go further it is worth drawing attention to two Biblical texts, and a third from Justin Martyr[4], which all refer to the reading of Scripture in Christian synagogues.

In the first of these the Revelation of John concludes its preface as follows: "Happy is the man who *reads*, and happy those who *listen* to the words of this prophecy and heed what is written in it" (Revelation 1.3). Read casually, this could be taken to suggest that you can either read the Revelation of John for yourself, or have someone read it to you. But the reading and the listening are simultaneous. The reading referred to is the *public* reading of Scripture in a Christian service. And it would appear (its author says so) that the Revelation of John was *specifically* written to provide such readings.

The First Letter to Timothy is of similar date (AD c.100), notwithstanding its attribution to Paul, and includes the following injunction: "Until I arrive devote your attention to the *public reading of scriptures*, to exhortation, and to teaching" (1 Timothy 4.13). The reference to Scripture may, or may not, include Christian Scripture, but at the least it confirms that

Christian synagogues continued to follow the traditional Jewish cycle of readings. Exhortation and teaching appear to have followed.

By the middle of the second century readings from Scripture had become common at Christian Eucharists and Justin Martyr (*c.*100–*c.*165) suggests that too many readings can hold things up. He wrote in his Apology: "And on the day which is called the day of the sun there is an assembly of all who live in the towns or in the country; and the memoirs of the Apostles or the writings of the prophets are read, *as long as time permits*" (Apology 1.67). The "Memoirs of the Apostles" (the Gospels, presumably) would have had precedence and would have been read last. But Old Testament readings, perhaps, could be shortened. And progressively, as observance of the Jewish Sabbath lapsed, so too did the scrupulous observance of the Jewish lectionary and calendar.

Mark's Cycle of Readings

We need, next, to explore more exactly how the Gospels correlate with the Jewish calendar of festivals and fasts.

The one fixed point in any Christian Lectionary is Passover, since it is the anniversary of the Crucifixion and Resurrection. It is the one specifically Christian anniversary and we know from Mark's Gospel that it was commemorated by a vigil. Mark's church will, therefore, almost certainly have read his last *pericope*, the story of the Empty Tomb (Mark 16. 1-8), on Easter Day. But since Passover is commemorated for eight days from *15th* Nisan, which is already two weeks into the Jewish cycle of Torah readings, the two cycles (Christian and Jewish) could never match exactly. The Jewish calendar took no account of Christian anniversaries, but Mark certainly will have done. The Passion Narrative is the climax of his Gospel and he will have located his closing *pericope* on the third Sabbath in Nisan.

Although Mark himself will not have written his Gospel in this way, *our* best tactic in trying to discover what he has done, is to hook this last *pericope* on to the third Sabbath in Nisan, and then unroll his Gospel *backwards*, like a carpet. There is no real problem in identifying his individual readings (they are, as we have seen, "like beads on a string") but it will soon become apparent that there are not enough of them to take us back to the beginning of the year. Mark's Gospel, therefore, cannot have provided readings for *every* Sunday. So, assuming that it was Mark's intention to provide *weekly* readings, it must have been his intention to begin on the other Jewish New Year (1st Tishri). He would then have provided readings for six months, from October to mid-April.

We now look for landfalls - Festivals or Sabbaths where Mark's reading so exactly fits the theme of that Sabbath or Festival that it cannot be a coincidence. We should not expect a correspondence every Sabbath (Mark had other concerns), but the Festivals must be right, since Mark could hardly disregard them. And this will quickly be put to the test since Tishri begins with a cluster of festivals - New Year on 1st Tishri, the Day of Atonement on 10th Tishri, and Tabernacles (an eight day festival) on 15th Tishri.

The theme of Jewish New Year is the coming of God's reign, which people must await, in penitence and in joyful anticipation. So Mark's Gospel begins with John the Baptist's call to penitence and Jesus' arrival in Galilee, amidst great excitement, proclaiming the coming Kingdom of God (Mark 1. 1-20). The Day of Atonement in Jesus' day had an elaborate ritual and was a day of corporate penitence. Again Mark's stories of the Paralytic, of Levi, and of Jesus associating with "bad characters - tax-gatherers and others" (Mark 2. 1-22) provides a perfect Christian fulfilment. For Jesus himself can forgive sins and there is no longer any need for the rituals prescribed in Leviticus. And so on to Tabernacles, one of the original pilgrim festivals. Here again Mark's reading is appropriate to the occasion. It was an eight-day festival and in Mark 3.7 - 4.34 he provides eight readings. The "great numbers" who attend Jesus reflect the Tabernacles theme of Israel's being joined by the nations at the end of the world (Zechariah 14.16). Then, as Moses had done, Jesus calls twelve men to represent the new Israel, the church. And finally, in a series of harvest parables (Tabernacles was originally a harvest festival), Jesus illustrates different facets of God's kingdom (Mark 4. 1-34).

159

The next festival is Hanukkah, which was celebrated for eight days from 25th Kislev onwards, that is about two months later. And Mark again provides eight readings, although not a discourse (Mark 7.1 - 9.29), which are appropriate to the occasion. Hanukkah commemorates the re-building and purification of the temple in Jerusalem by Judas Maccabeus in 164 BC. The story is told in 2 Maccabees 2. It was believed that God's glory cloud had left the temple, when it was destroyed in 586 BC, and now at Hanukkah its return is celebrated. The story of the Transfiguration, therefore, is particularly appropriate (Mark 9. 2-8). God's glory cloud, the symbol of his presence, now descends upon Jesus, as it had upon Moses when he ascended Mount Sinai, upon Elijah on Mount Horeb, and upon the temple in Jerusalem on its rededication.

As regards the weekly cycle of readings, Mark inclines to follow the Elijah and Elisha cycle of Haphtarah readings, rather than those from the Torah, as I have already shown in the chapter on Mark's Gospel.

Matthew's Cycle of Readings

We do not know why Mark's Gospel only provided readings for the six months from Jewish New Year in Tishri (October), but it must have left his church without readings from mid-April to September. It may not have been the only reason which prompted Matthew to re-write Mark, but it was a practical need which he will have wanted to address. His Gospel, therefore, is longer than Mark's (twenty-eight chapters to sixteen) primarily because he has added further lections (sixty-eight in all against Mark's fifty-six) to provide readings for *every* Sabbath in the year, as well as for additional festivals.

The chapter on the Gospel according to Matthew has already set out the five discourses (Matthew 5-7, 10.5 - 11.1, 13. 1-53, 18 and 24-25) and shown how they correlate with the themes of successive Jewish festivals. Matthew's reading for Pentecost (Matthew 5-7), which falls in the period not covered by Mark, is the Sermon on the Mount. His discourse for New Year (Matthew 10.5 - 11.1) is the commissioning of the Twelve. Their ministry, effectively, is an extension of Jesus' ministry, which had been Mark's reading. His discourse for Tabernacles

(Matthew 13) is an expansion of Mark's (Mark 4), and his reading for Hanukkah is, again, Mark's reading (the Transfiguration), but followed by a discourse as well (Matthew 18). And, finally (we would now expect this), his discourse for Passover (Matthew 24-25) is, yet again, Mark's discourse (Mark 13), but extended with additional parables.

Matthew's Gospel, like Mark's, is also committed to the *weekly* readings prescribed in the Jewish Lectionary and he tends to favour the Torah readings. Passover begins on 15th Nisan, midway through the month, and it would be reasonable to suppose that Matthew's church began reading his Gospel on the first Sabbath in Iyyar (the following month). The four Torah readings for Iyyar are from Genesis 23 - 36 and tell the story of Abraham and Isaac, and of Isaac's two sons, Jacob and Esau. These chapters are rich in genealogies (the second reading is actually called "the Descendants") and Matthew follows them by beginning with Jesus' Table of Descent. Then, as the chapter on the Birth Narratives explains, the rivalry between Jacob and Esau (Genesis 27 - 28) provided the idea for the rivalry between Herod and Jesus. Herod was another Esau and Jesus another Jacob.

Mark's Gospel had no appropriate reading for Purim on 11th Adar, but Matthew's Gospel does. Purim celebrated the deliverance of the Jews from Persian rule and the readings were from Esther. Esther 7 describes a royal banquet, which King Ahasuerus gives for his Jewish wife, Esther, who takes advantage of the occasion to denounce Haman as the principal scourge of the Jews. Haman is ultimately hanged on the very scaffold which he had himself set up for the execution of a devout Jew, Mordecai. Matthew first retells Mark's parable of the Vineyard, or Wicked Husbandmen, much of it word for word (Mark 12. 1-12; Matthew 21. 33-46), and then midrashes it with the Esther story in the parable of the Wedding Feast (Matthew 22. 1-14). Where, in Mark's parable, God is the owner of the Vineyard, in Matthew's parable of the Wedding Feast he is a king who invites guests (his tenants, the Jews) to the wedding of his son, Jesus. Jesus' disciples are the guests at the wedding, and those who refuse the invitation are the tenants in Mark's parable who refuse to pay the rent. So Christians are invited, but one comes improperly dressed (unrepentant) and he suffers the misfortune of the wretched Haman. We may not think it a very edifying parable, but Matthew believed that no one should take heaven for granted and thought it better that we should be warned.

Luke's Cycle of Readings

Luke follows the Sabbath readings set out in the Jewish Lectionary quite as diligently as Mark and Matthew, but he has few readings that are specific to the festivals, and we must assume that he wrote his Gospel for a predominantly non-Jewish, and possibly Pauline church. A congregation that did not observe Pentecost, New Year, Tabernacles, and Hanukkah would not have found Matthew's Gospel appropriate. So, while we can assume that Luke's Gospel, like Matthew's, was written to provide a series of lections throughout the year (it has a suitable number of *pericope*), there are not the landfalls that anchored Mark and Matthew to the Jewish festal calendar.

Luke also did not quite have the freedom that Mark and Matthew enjoyed, since he is conflating their Gospels and that in itself imposed a constraint. In general, therefore, a correspondence with the weekly Torah reading is more likely where he is a free spirit, that is in the Birth Narratives and in the Lukan Journey (Luke 9.51 - 18.14). But there is also evidence that Luke was aware of the Haphtarah readings from the Deuteronomic History cycle (Joshua - 2 Kings), and from Isaiah, Job, and Ecclesiasticus.

It is less clear how John's Gospel was read. The Pauline churches were, in general, against all things Jewish and it is most unlikely that they followed the weekly or festal cycles of the Jewish year. Such clues as we have (the repeated references in John's Gospel to "three days later", or "a week later") may indicate it was read over a period of seven weeks, perhaps the seven weeks before Easter (Lent as we know it today), but we cannot be sure.

The Modern Lectionary

The traditional Christian liturgical year begins on the fourth Sunday before Christmas (Advent 1), but the Lectionary provided for use with the modern Anglican Prayer Book, Common Worship, begins five weeks earlier, on the 9th Sunday before Christmas. It provides for a triennial cycle of Sunday readings - Year A, Year B, and Year C. Year A was the prescribed cycle for the year beginning on Advent Sunday 2001. Very similar cycles are used in other churches. It is an advance on the two-yearly cycle prescribed for use with the Alternative Service Book (1980-2000) but remains seriously deficient in almost every respect.

For the sad truth is that the reading of Scripture today is a relatively minor component of any service. Fewer and fewer churches even have a Lectern Bible (a Missal with just the prescribed readings is often thought sufficient) and the readings are very short (commonly with fewer than ten verses, sometimes as few as five). Whole swathes of the New Testament are never read.

A lectionary needs to be flexible because any cycle of readings will have to be broken from time to time by festivals, special occasions, and the seasons of Advent and Lent. They can, however, accommodate such interruptions by resuming afterwards at the place where they left off. My own practice, throughout my forty-year ministry, was to read the books of the New Testament more or less in their entirety from beginning to end in lections of about twenty verses. The Gospels would take a year or so to read (Mark and John a little less), so that a complete cycle of Gospel readings would take about four years. But, most importantly, there was no jumping around. We did not read Mark one week, Luke the next, and John the next. Readings from one of the three longer Pauline Epistles, the Letter to the Hebrews, and the Revelation of John might occupy perhaps three or four months. Different sections of the Acts of the Apostles were read for three months or so after Pentecost each year, so that most of Acts would be read over a four-year period. There were also short series of special readings for Advent and Lent.

The Old Testament presents a particular problem. The Common Worship lectionary includes an Old Testament reading for every week, but the readings are quite short so that there are, inevitably, a disproportionate number of readings from the Prophets. *Stories* are much more characteristic of the Old Testament than prophecies, but stories demand longer readings than the Common Worship lectionary allows and so they are less frequently read. My practice was to read books of the Old Testament and Apocrypha in sequence at Evening Prayer and a complete cycle of Old Testament readings might then take perhaps eight or ten years to complete. But we did have Morning Prayer once a month, in place of a Sung Eucharist, and we then had a single Old Testament reading of some length from whatever book was being read in the evening. Congregations can only expect to take in two readings at most in a single service.

The practice described above has a huge number of advantages. First and foremost, by reading books in their entirety, chapter by chapter, congregations are helped to understand the particular perspective and outlook of each Gospel or Letter. The four Gospels are not all alike and their integrity is compromised when only selected passages are read, mixed in with other readings and out of order. Neglected and seemingly irrelevant passages can often be crucial to our understanding of an individual book. We should not need to have the Gospels edited for us.

A congregation's understanding of a reading will also be helped by a service sheet which includes a short summary of each reading and a little background information about it. Many churches today print the lessons out, which is mistaken. The public reading of a Gospel or Epistle is a performance, and congregations should not bury their heads in their service sheets any more than a theatre audience should do at the performance of a play. It is better to attend to the live performance, which can help our understanding of it, and study the text at home afterwards.

Another significant advantage is that a preacher is not confronted by the same text every three years and left wondering what there is new to say. Instead there is the stimulation of a new text every week, without the need to explain its context because it will follow on from the previous week's reading. My experience of churchgoing since retirement has confirmed that preachers often look upon the lessons for the

Sunday in question with dismay and find no real inspiration in them.

Since retiring I have also come across an innovation in New Zealand, which I would have wished to follow, were I still at my old church. Lessons should be introduced by referring to the chapter and verse of the book from which they are taken (it is now fashionable, for some reason, to leave these out) and the end can be marked with the words: "Hear what this reading says to the church". To my mind this is much more appropriate than "This is the Word of the Lord", because it does not absolutely endorse what has been read (we may disagree with part of it), and instead simply invites us to reflect upon the *relevance* of the reading.

This has proved a longer chapter than I anticipated, but no issue could be more important for the church than the reading and understanding of Scripture.

[1] This chapter draws heavily upon *Midrash and Lection in Matthew* (SPCK 1974) and *The Evangelists' Calendar, A Lectionary Explanation of the Development of Scripture* (SPCK 1978), both of them by Michael Goulder.

[2] It may be helpful to include an explanation of some of the technical words that are commonly encountered in connection with the liturgical reading of Jewish Scripture:

Torah means "Law" in Hebrew and refers not just to the Law in the narrow sense, but to all the first five books of the Old Testament from Genesis to Deuteronomy. The Torah reading for any individual Sabbath is known as the sidrôt.

The second, prophetic reading is known as the Haphtarah ("the closer" in Hebrew), indicating that it brings the service to an end.

Targum is Hebrew for "translation", and originally referred to the Aramaic translation that followed the reading of the Torah and Haphtarah in Hebrew, in synagogues where Hebrew was not understood.

Mishnah means "instruction" in Hebrew, and various Mishnah supplemented the Torah reading by classifying the Jewish law under six headings. It represents the development of Scripture and claims to represent an oral tradition as old as Scripture. The most famous of these Mishnah is attributed to Rabbi Judah the Prince and dates from around AD c.200.

The Talmud (literally "study" in Hebrew) includes the Mishnah of Rabbi Judah, together with subsequent commentaries upon it in Aramaic, known as Gemara (Gemara is Aramaic for "completion").

The Jerusalem, or Palestinian, Talmud dates from the fourth century, and the Babylonian Talmud from the sixth century AD.

[3] The Preface to Ecclesiasticus (literally the Church Book, so called because it appealed to Christians and was read in church) or (its proper name) the Wisdom of Jesus ben Sirach, several times refers to "the law, the prophets, and *the writers who followed in their steps*". He was one such himself, a Scribe, and intended his book to be read in the synagogue as a *third* lesson. The Wisdom Literature is known collectively as the Writings.

[4] Justin Martyr (*c.*100–*c.*165) was a Greek philosopher, who embraced Christianity when he was about thirty and founded schools of Christian learning in Ephesus and Rome. He was concerned to show that Christianity was a reasonable faith and wrote two books, his *First* and *Second Apology*, addressed to the Emperor, Senate and wider Roman world, explaining what Christians believed and did. He was denounced as a Christian by the Cynic philosopher, Crescens, refused to offer a sacrifice to the gods, and was scourged and beheaded. An account of his death survives.

The Jewish Calendar in New Testament Times

	Festival	*Reading*	*Theme*
14th Nisan (8 days)	Passover (Pesah)	Exodus 12	The Exodus from Egypt
6th Sivan	Pentecost (Shabuoth)	Exodus 20	The Law Giving on Mount Sinai
9th Ab	9th Ab	Lamentations	A fast commemorating the destruction of Jerusalem in 586 BC
1st Tishri	New Year (Rosh Hashshanah)	Genesis 21-22	The hope that God will establish a New Age
10th Tishri	Day of Atonement (Yom Kippur)	Leviticus 16 and 18	The Day of Judgement
15th Tishri (8 days)	Tabernacles (Sukkoth)	Leviticus 22 - 24	The building of the Temple (and autumn festival)
25th Chislev	Hanukkah	2 Maccabees	The descent of the Shekinah (God's glory cloud) upon the Temple (and the winter solstice)
11th Adar	Purim	Esther	The deliverance of the Jews from exile

Passover, Pentecost and Tabernacles are known as Pilgrim Festivals. In the days of the monarchy, before the conquest of the Northern Kingdom (*c.*1,000-722 BC), all Israel gathered, with full military honours, at traditional shrines (Bethel, Dan, Shechem and others). But with the fall of Samaria this was no longer possible and the festivals were thereafter celebrated in Jerusalem.

There are two New Years in the Jewish Calendar, 1st Nisan and 1st Tishri. 1st Nisan, which falls around the end of March, is the older of the two and the Torah readings revolve around it. So, on the last Sabbath in Adar (the last month of the year), Deuteronomy 33 – 34 is read. And then on the following Sabbath, the 1st Sabbath in Nisan, the cycle begins again with Genesis 1 – 6.8. But 1st Tishri, which falls around the beginning of October, is celebrated as New Year proper

The exact reconstruction of the Lectionary is both problematical and controversial. The readings listed above are purely indicative.

TWO OLD TESTAMENT TEXTS

INTRODUCTION

If this Handbook is successful, I am hoping, ultimately, to add three others on Old Testament texts, post Biblical texts (Creeds and Liturgies) and on outstanding Christian authors (from Eusebius of Caesarea to Albert Schweitzer). However, this will take time and I therefore thought to include, in this first Handbook, chapters on two of the most often quoted, and most misunderstood, of all Old Testament texts - the Creation Stories and the Ten Commandments. As Fact Sheets they were always in demand on the Bookstall of my old church and I had many, many times to run off further copies.

The first Creation story, in particular, has had an enormous influence upon our understanding of the world and of our place within it. Few people in this country believe that it is literally true, but it still shapes our beliefs, and references to "God's creation" are as common today as they ever were.

In the same way appeal is often made to the Ten Commandments. We may no longer be able to remember them all, but the idea of simple, unambiguous standards of morality remains attractive. So this text, too, deserves particularly careful study.

THE CREATION STORIES

So strong has been the impact of the first Creation Story (Genesis 1.1 - 2.3) that the second story (Genesis 2.4 - 3.24) has often been overlooked. But they are easily distinguished. The first uses the word "Yahweh" for God ("Jehovah", or simply "God" in the New English Bible translation), while the second uses the word "Elohim" (translated "the Lord God"). When studied carefully they can be seen to give different (in fact, conflicting) descriptions of how the world began.

The First Creation Story

The most obvious feature of the first Creation Story is its artificial division of creation into six days. There are, in fact, eight acts of creation so that the third and sixth days are each allocated two:

Day 1	God creates light and separates it from darkness, creating day and night (Genesis 1. 1-5)
Day 2	God creates the vault of heaven, separating the waters above the vault from those beneath it (Genesis 1. 6-8)
Day 3	God gathers the waters beneath the vault, creating dry land and seas (Genesis 1. 9-10) God creates plants bearing seeds, and trees bearing fruit (Genesis 1. 11-13)
Day 4	God creates the sun, moon, and stars to serve as signs for festivals and seasons, and to divide day and night (Genesis 1. 14-19)
Day 5	God creates sea creatures and birds (Genesis 1. 20-23)
Day 6	God creates the land creatures (Genesis 1. 24-25) God creates man in his own image to rule over his created world (Genesis 1. 26-31)
Day 7	God rests and ordains the Sabbath as a holy day (Genesis 2. 1-3)

The *primary* purpose of this first Creation Story is *religious* - to show that the Sabbath is divinely ordained. God himself rested on the Sabbath, and Sabbath observance, therefore, is incumbent upon us as well. *We* must do as *God* did. But the sun and moon also serve a religious purpose (it is their *raison d'être*). They may separate day and night but, more importantly, they "serve as signs both for festivals and for seasons and years". The phases of the moon, in particular, determine when Passover, Pentecost, New Year, and Tabernacles are celebrated, and are the basis of the Jewish lunar year of either twelve or thirteen months.

The story is liturgical in character and its author belonged to the Priestly School of writers, who were the final editors of the Old Testament and contributed the Books of Numbers and Leviticus, 1 and 2 Chronicles, Ezra and Nehemiah. As their name suggests, they were principally interested in the liturgical aspects of Judaism (there were no longer kings or prophets) and in the observance of the Law in all its minute detail. They put their story first, not because it was older, but because they thought it sounder. It is the privilege of an editor.

The author of this first Creation Story, therefore, is not interested in the natural world for its own sake. His story is based, not upon observation, but upon a much older tradition embodied in Psalm 104:

Genesis 1-2	Psalm 104
God creates light	O Lord my God, thou art great indeed, clothed in majesty and splendour, and wrapped in a robe of light (Psalm 104. 1-2)
God creates the vault of heaven	Thou spreadest out the heavens like a tent and on their waters laid the beams of thy pavilion (Psalm 104. 2-3). Thou didst fix the earth on its foundation. The deep overspread it like a cloak (Psalm 104. 5-6).
God creates dry land	The waters lay above the mountains. At thy rebuke they ran, at the sound of thy thunder they rushed away (Psalm 104. 7-8). The gullies, in particular, are a hospitable place for wild animals and birds (Psalm 104. 10-12).

God creates grass and trees	Thou makest grass grow for the cattle and green things for those who toil for man (Psalm 104.14).
God creates the sun and moon	Thou hast made the moon to measure the year and taught the sun where to set (Psalm 104.19). The night brings out the nocturnal animals. The day belongs to man. The earth is full of God's creatures, beasts great and small (Psalm 104. 20-24).
God creates the sea creatures	The immeasurable sea is also home to numberless creatures (Psalm 104. 25-26).
	All animals look to God for food and life, and are entirely dependent upon him (Psalm 104. 27-30).
God rests on the seventh day	May the glory of the Lord stand for ever and may he rejoice in his works (Psalm 104. 31-end).

The Second Creation Story

The second Creation Story is on a more modest and much less cosmic scale. God is thought of as a rather kindly father figure and the author reflects upon the oddness of life.

God forms man from the dust of the ground and breathes into his nostrils the breath of life. God plants a garden in Eden and sets the man in it. In the middle of the garden are two trees - the tree of life and the tree of the knowledge of good and evil (Genesis 2. 4-9).
The geography of the known world (Genesis 2. 10-14)
Man is set to work in the garden. He must not eat from the tree of the knowledge of good and evil. But man is lonely, so God creates wild animals and birds to keep him company. Finally he takes one of the man's ribs to create woman. There is a verse to explain this and the origin of her name (Genesis 2. 15-25).

> The woman is betrayed by the serpent, and the man by the woman, into eating from the tree of the knowledge of good and evil. Their eyes are opened and they make themselves clothes to hide their shame (Genesis 3. 1-7).

> The man and the woman are found out (Genesis 3. 8-14).

> God gives out the punishments. The serpent will be legless and will be distrusted by man. The woman will give birth in pain and will be subservient to her husband. The man is condemned to a daily round of unrewarding work and to a life that will end in death (Genesis 3. 9-19).

> Adam and Eve are given their names and are expelled from the garden of Eden into the real world (Genesis 3. 20-24).

This second story is known as an aetiological tale, because it seeks to explain the origin or cause of things that are odd or puzzling - why the sexes are different, why human beings wear clothes, why snakes have no legs, why women experience pain in childbirth, why men are the dominant sex, why farming is such hard work, and, above all, the origin of death. The story is simply, even naively, written and we would describe it today as a folk story.

Most obviously, the two stories are inconsistent. In the first Creation Story God creates the world and only then sets man within it. In the second he creates Adam first and then assembles the world around him like a tableau. The first story has a cosmic dimension. The second is on a much more human scale. It also has no interest in Sabbath observance or in religious festivals. Instead the story explains the parameters and realities of human life – how things came to be as they are.

The Stories Scientifically Assessed

Neither story was intended to give an accurate scientific account of what happened at the beginning of the world. The interest of the first story is primarily religious (to show that the Sabbath is divinely ordained), while the second is written to satisfy human curiosity (to explain the "funny old world" we live in).

From a strictly scientific point of view the stories are mistaken in several respects:

(1) Both stories portray the world as a static place, where everything has always been as it is. In fact we know it to be a changing world. Over millions of years climatic conditions have altered and new species have evolved. Others have become extinct. And it is still changing. The Earth is not a stable place.

(2) Neither story recognises the scale of things. There is no conception of the solar system, or of the galaxies, or of the time span involved. Famously, Archbishop Ussher (1581-1656) calculated, from the Biblical evidence, that God had created the world in the year 4004 BC. All but fundamentalist Christians think that it is somewhat older.

(3) Both stories portray man as being different in kind from the animal kingdom and as the crown or centrepiece of creation. As they are told, God makes the world for man's sake. Yet we now know that we are very recent arrivals on the world scene, animals ourselves, and the product of evolution. So it is a purely human conceit that we are superior to other animals and that they exist only to serve our purposes.

Modern Understandings of the World

In conclusion it may be helpful to re-state how present day scientists view the world and the process by which it has evolved. It is based on observation and evidence[1].

The blue sky above us is misleading because we are seeing everything through the earth's atmosphere. Most of the universe is empty black space - in fact, 99.999998% of it. There are no "waters above the firmament".

Our earth is not the centre of the universe but one of the sun's seven larger satellites, or planets. The sun itself is just a medium sized star, but it looks so big because it is very near - only 93 million miles away. The next nearest star is 25 million million miles away and its light takes four years to reach us. The moon, while the largest object in the sky, is tiny in cosmic terms, and indeed smaller than the earth. Its light is the sun's reflected light and its phases, so significant in Jewish religion, are caused by its revolving around the earth.

The stars that are visible to the naked eye (and millions that are not) form a single galaxy called the Milky Way. We have given it that name because, on a dark night, and seen from where we see it, it looks like milk poured across the sky from north to south. But the Milky Way is only one of many such galaxies, each with as many stars again. The next nearest galaxy to ours is more than 12 million million million (12,000,000,000,000,000,000) miles away. Through a telescope it looks like a Catherine Wheel. Even the light from this nearest galaxy takes thousands of years to reach us. We are seeing it as it was before the time of Jesus.

And everything in the world, everything, is revolving and dispersing. The residual heat of the explosion, which caused all this, is still measurable.

This is very roughly the time scale within which these things are thought to have happened:

An explosion of unimaginable size and impact took place (Big Bang)	14,000,000,000 years ago
The earth was formed	4,600,000,000 years ago
The earliest forms of life appeared	3,300,000,000 years ago
The dinosaurs appeared	193,000,000 years ago
The earliest forms of human life date from	100,000 years ago
The Ice Age ended	12,000 years ago
The first human civilisations appeared	10,000 years ago
Jesus lived	2,000 years ago
The Scientific and Industrial Revolutions began	250 years ago
We are living	Now

And the process continues. We have no idea at what point in the cycle or process we are.

In Conclusion

It is a curious thing that Christian faith is still bugged by the first Creation Story, and that it is still often taught in schools as literal truth, when we know it to be scientifically mistaken. Some people argue that there is time enough, as children grow older, to correct any mistaken ideas, but it is surely better to encourage them from the outset to look down a microscope or telescope, and see things for themselves, as they are.

But adult thinking, too, is still shaped by the story. Christians commonly speak of "the Creation" when they mean "the world", and the Apostles' Creed describes God as "the Maker of heaven and earth", when it was never "made" in the ordinary sense of the word. It would really be more accurate to describe the present world as "the Evolution", although that could be misleading as well. I simply make the point that the words "Creator" and "Creation" derive from the stories in Genesis 1 - 3 and will always carry echoes of those stories, however mistaken we now think them to be. They have created a mindset, which still lives on and perpetuates the original misunderstanding.

None of this would matter if it were not without contemporary relevance. It is difficult today to appreciate the hysteria that surrounded Galileo's discovery that the earth revolved around the sun, nor the publication of Darwin's *Origin of Species*. It is as if the Creation Stories have prevented Christians from welcoming the unfolding truth about our world and ourselves. Instead every advance has been marked by protest and compromise.

In the last 100 years, a huge number of people have discovered an interest in the natural world, and recognise the need for conservation, both in terms of preserving wildlife and in terms of conserving precious, non-renewable natural resources. Conservation societies like the Royal Society for the Protection of Birds, with more than a million members in the United Kingdom, are amongst the most dynamic groups within our society. Twentieth century Christian beliefs must reflect these concerns, and a commitment to goals which people, in Biblical times, could not have understood. The world is not ours to exploit and destroy as we wish. We are not a superior species. For all their interest, ancient stories cannot be allowed to define how we understand the world today.

¹ There are obviously many books about astronomy, but I have taken my information from Dr Stuart Malin's *Stars, Galaxies and Nebulae*, which was published in 1989 in the Greenwich Guide series. Stuart, who is a good friend, is a geophysicist and astronomer and, at the time, was Head of Astronomy at the Old Royal Observatory, Greenwich.

THE TEN COMMANDMENTS

After the Reformation the Ten Commandments (with the Lord's Prayer and the Apostles' Creed) were often painted on the walls of Church of England churches. It is a measure of the authority they once had as a standard of morality.

The Text

The text of the Ten Commandments is found in Exodus 20 and Deuteronomy 5. There are no very significant differences between the two versions, but Exodus is the older book. Deuteronomy (literally the "Second Law") is really a collection of discourses on the Law, expounding their meaning and urging their observance. There is also another similar table of eight commandments in Exodus 34. But for Jewish people, not just the Ten Commandments but the whole of the Pentateuch (Genesis, Exodus, Leviticus, Numbers and Deuteronomy) is the Law (the Torah) and no part of it has any greater or lesser authority. The Ten Commandments are therefore only a small part of the Law. The Law, in its entirety, regulates every aspect of Jewish life. In Judaism the giving of God's Law to Moses on Mount Sinai is celebrated at Pentecost, when Exodus 19-20 is read.

In summary the Ten Commandments are:

1	You shall have no other God.
2	You shall not make carved images.
3	You shall not mis-use God's name.
4	Remember to keep the Sabbath day holy.
5	Honour your father and your mother.
6	You shall not commit murder.
7	You shall not commit adultery.
8	You shall not steal.
9	You shall not give false evidence.
10	You shall not covet.

By tradition they were written on two tablets of stone, to distinguish the first four commandments (our duty to God) from the second six (our duty to other people). But they are not unique. A number of legal codes were inscribed on stone in the second millennium BC and have survived to this day. Some are in the British Museum, but the most famous, the Code of Hammurabi, the eighteenth century BC Amorite king of Babylon, is in the Louvre in Paris.

The Individual Commandments

In the past the authority of the Ten Commandments has rested upon their being part of Scripture. They were believed to have been handed by God to Moses on Mount Sinai. On this view they remain of equal truth, validity, and authority for all time and in all places. This is the view that is taken by the author of Exodus himself, by orthodox Jews, and by Christians of conservative outlook. But a careful study of the Ten Commandments reveals them to be, as we might expect, very much of their time and place.

The first commandment assumes the existence of other gods. What is commanded is loyalty to *YHWH*, Yahweh, the God of Israel.

The second commandment refers to the "waters under the earth" (an ancient misunderstanding of what the world was once like) and implies that God is vindictive and punishes, not only those fathers who break it, but their children, grandchildren and great grandchildren as well.

The fourth commandment enjoins Sabbath observance, which means from sunset on Friday to sunset on Saturday and, like the first Creation Story, assumes that the world was created in six days. The degrees of inferiority, too, (sons, daughters, slaves, slave-girls, cattle and foreigners) all belong to the past.

The reward for honouring father and mother is "to live long in the land which the Lord your God is giving you". It is a reward which will only appeal to Jewish people, and not to all of them.

The sixth, seventh, eighth and ninth commandments are models of brevity and are what most people have in mind when they appeal to the Ten Commandments. But there are pitfalls for the incautious. In the 1980s Conservative Members of Parliament in the United Kingdom commonly cited the Ten Commandments, with the sixth very much in mind (they took a strong line on law and order). But they overlooked the seventh, which many of them broke.

The final commandment confirms, what we might have suspected, that the Ten Commandments as a whole are addressed to men. Only men attended synagogue services or went on pilgrim festivals. So this commandment lists a *man's* possessions - his house, his wife, his slave, his slave girl, his ox, his ass and then anything else. There is nothing here for women to do, or not do, except "be possessed"!

The Authority of the Ten Commandments

Most of those who argue for the absolute authority of the Ten Commandments today read them selectively. Their appeal lies in their being so categorically against murder, adultery, theft and lying. But what of the other commandments, and the beliefs and values that underlie them? Who today, except Jewish people, believes that we should observe Saturday as a holy day? Or that God punishes a man's great grandchildren for things that he has done? Or that the world was made in six days? Or that only men are moral, and that a woman can be included amongst a man's possessions? Or that living in Israel is a fitting reward for honouring your parents? Or that slavery is defensible?

All of these things were accepted by Jewish people in the ninth or eighth-century BC, and who can quarrel with them? Every culture and every century has had its own values, which seemed right at the time. But many of these values and beliefs are now thought wrong or mistaken. It leads us inexorably to a conclusion, which those of a conservative outlook will always resist, that all morality is relative to the people and circumstances it addresses. There is not a single, universal standard of right and wrong written down anywhere. Only *we* can be the judges of right and wrong, and people will differ in their view. The very fact that the Ten Commandments are read selectively shows that they are no longer universal divine imperatives.

Christian Re-interpretations

Every generation, therefore, has to re-interpret morality for itself. And this was true even of the early church. Many of them were Jewish Christians, who were used to celebrating the Law-Giving at Pentecost. But now that they were Christian Jews, what should they celebrate? Not the giving of the Law to *Moses*, but *the re-interpretation* of that law in the teaching of Jesus. So Matthew has Jesus ascend another mount (a theological rather than a physical one) to deliver a new law, a new Ten Commandments for Christians.

By contrast Luke's Church was predominantly non-Jewish. There is evidence that they no longer observed the Jewish calendar as strictly as Matthew's church did, if at all. So what should they celebrate at Pentecost? They lived, not by the Law, but by the Spirit. Let Pentecost, therefore, be a festival of the Holy Spirit. This was Luke's suggestion (Acts 2) and he wrote his story accordingly.

Morality, or ethics, can be studied historically, and the Ten Commandments, with other ancient codes like the Hippocratic Oath, will always occupy the early chapters of such a study. But every subject progresses and the challenge we face is to apply our Christian core values (faithfulness, courage, compassion, integrity, penitence, generosity, truthfulness) to the distinctive contemporary issues which most concern us today - human rights, poverty, environmental issues, personal relationships, race and gender.

APPENDICES

MICHAEL GOULDER - A TRIBUTE

Michael Goulder's name recurs again and again throughout this Handbook, yet many readers may never have heard of him. He was for many years the Extra-Mural Lecturer in Theology at Birmingham University, but was never offered a professorship at Oxford, his old university, although he five times gave the Speaker's Lectures there and was awarded a D.D. (Doctor of Divinity), the University's highest degree.

In some ways, however, Birmingham has suited Michael because although he has been denied the PhD students, who might have worked with him, he was relatively free of administrative duties, has written a succession of scholarly books and articles, and has won an enviable international reputation. All the books, and two of the articles he has written, are listed at the end of this chapter.

But today, in retirement, Michael is confined to a wheel chair after a series of disabling strokes. He is as stoical and cheerful as he has always been since contracting polio in childhood, but his eyesight is also very poor now and he cannot read. He delivered what will probably prove to be his last lecture at the University without notes. And, disappointingly for me, he is unable to read this book. He would certainly have improved it.

My Own Involvement With Michael

I first came across Michael while reading theology at Oxford. His very first article, co-written with M.L.Sanderson, appeared in the *Journal of Theological Studies* in April 1957. It was entitled "St Luke's Genesis" and I noted it at length - eight closely written sides of foolscap in my student handwriting of fifty years ago. I had no idea at the time who Michael was, and was not to come across him again, and then only by chance, until some eight years later. But this article was completely convincing.

In all, over a period of some thirty-five years, Michael was to write eleven books, twenty-nine articles, forty-six book reviews, contribute nineteen essays to multi-author works, and deliver many, many lectures, often and most recently to international conferences of Biblical scholars. This makes him one of the most productive professional biblical scholars of the late twentieth century and he is quite unusual in being equally at home in both Old and New Testament studies, and in early Church History. Key to this is his (to me) amazing command of languages - Hebrew, Aramaic, Greek and Latin, as well as modern European languages. And, sadly, he had many more books in him, which will now never be written.

All of Michael's books, however, except possibly his next to last, *A Tale of Two Missions*, were written for fellow professionals and are more or less inaccessible to the ordinary reader. None ever went into a second edition and all are out of print today. His name is hardly ever to be found in the bibliography of other academic books and until recently he has had few professional English supporters. A notable exception is Dr Mark Goodacre[1], until recently a younger colleague of Michael's at Birmingham University, whose PhD thesis was entitled *Goulder and the Gospels*.

In 1965 I was awarded a curate, Alan Davis, and as part of his post-ordination training, he had to attend lectures at Birmingham University by - Michael Goulder! So I went with him and, long after Alan had left, continued going to a small Biblical Seminar which Michael led on a weekday morning. It was a very exciting time. Real progress is rare in Biblical Studies and yet, almost every week, Michael had further developments to report.

Michael's Achievement

What then has been Michael's achievement? In the 1950s, and for decades before then, a position had been reached in Biblical Studies that can be likened to an uncompleted crossword puzzle in which many wrong answers have been entered. Crossword puzzles are not my own forte, but when the correct answer to a clue is discovered, it is self-evidently right. If there is any uncertainty, the answer is probably wrong. Every correct entry makes the remaining clues easier to solve (you have letters towards the answer you are seeking), while every wrong entry makes the completion of the puzzle more difficult. So, by the mid-1950s, when I read theology at Oxford, the puzzle was a complete mess. It was not obviously so to a young undergraduate, but the crossword was only half finished at best and no one had entered a new answer to a clue for a very long while. Some of the answers were written in ink, and some in pencil. New books were rewrites of old ones and, when anyone suggested scratching out any of the inked-in entries, as Austin Farrer did, they were quickly derided. It was bewildering to some (we were trying to *solve* the crossword puzzle and not trying to start it all over again), and it was hurtful to those whose solutions to individual clues had been accepted. Every author has a stake in any book they have written and the last thing an author wants is to see their contribution discarded.

On this analogy Michael has scratched out many of the inked-in entries as wrong and has thereby broken the deadlock. Suddenly the answers to other clues became apparent as well. There was a sort of landslide. To some, who had long studied the crossword, these developments were unwelcome and they chose to ignore them. But one test of a correct answer is its ability to help with the solution of other clues. And so, suddenly, progress was possible in every corner of the puzzle.

Dispensing with Q

It may be helpful, therefore, to explain the sequence of events and thereby Michael's contribution to Biblical Studies. The first incorrect answer to be whited out (a lot of Tipp-Ex was required and conservative scholars still keep on re-instating the wrong answer!) was Q. As explained in the chapter on the Synoptic Gospels, this was the non-existent, hypothetical, source which was said to underlie Matthew's and Luke's Gospels. Suddenly it was possible to think of the Synoptic Evangelists (Mark, Matthew and Luke) as authors in their own right and not as mindless copyists. Dispensing with Q was the key to it all, but in the face of scholarly opposition Michael has had to make the case again and again, and it therefore recurs in most of his books.

The next breakthrough was Michael's realisation that each of the Synoptic evangelists had his own perspective on the story of Jesus. If Mark's, Matthew's and Luke's Gospels are successive rewrites of one another, we can study their different versions of the same story in minute detail. We can then see how tiny glosses (the change of a single word, even) can help us recover their individual perspective on the story they are retelling. I do not know whether Michael was the very first to study the use of individual words in this way, but he was definitely the first to do so to any purpose. As a consequence of abandoning Q, therefore, we can now see the evangelists in a new light. They are creative authors - Scribes, as Matthew puts it. This introduced the concept of midrash, which had not before been associated with New Testament authors. It explains what guided them when they supplemented the Gospel, or Gospels, which they were expounding (Mark in Matthew's case, Mark and Matthew in Luke's) with material of their own.

The Lectionary Theory

Yet a further breakthrough then quickly followed. The challenge was to identify the purpose with which each of the evangelists wrote. What did they do with their Gospels, when they had written them? Why did they write them at all? Here nothing was inked in, although one or two tentative suggestions had been made. Michael's suggestion was that the Gospels were written for use in synagogue worship. They are Christian Scripture, provided for the church's use by Christian Scribes. A reading from one of the Synoptic Gospels, therefore, would follow the two readings from the Old Testament and would often have some relevance to it. But Michael's attempt to provide a *complete* reconstruction of the early Christian lectionary was perhaps overly ambitious and provided an easy target for criticism. Yet there is no doubt that he was thinking along the right lines. The Synoptic evangelists *did* intend their Gospels to be read as Scripture and the discourses in Mark's and Matthew's Gospels *do* fall naturally against the Jewish festivals. Some *pericope*, too, *do* seem appropriate to the *weekly* Sabbath readings, but not all of them. Life is never quite as tidy as that.

Michael's final major contribution to Biblical studies was to realise that the deep division within the church between Jewish and non-Jewish (Pauline) congregations was reflected in the New Testament. This was the theme of *A Tale of Two Missions*, and enabled him to place John's Gospel in context.

Michael's Present Standing

To conservative evangelical scholars Michael Goulder is a maverick and is ignored completely. Many liberal scholars, too, hanker after sources and, if any unresolved issue arises, regard the existence of Q and other hypothetical, written Gospel sources as the default, fall-back position. It has become the habit of a lifetime. It may also be that scholars of a conservative disposition have felt overwhelmed by so many new suggestions at once and so, rather than engage with them, carry on as if nothing has happened. Yet Michael's views are gaining ground. He has supporters amongst a younger generation of New Testament scholars and particularly overseas.

But my book is not intended for scholars, although I believe it to be scholarly. Scholars, in any case, have had every opportunity to grapple with Michael's views over some 30 years or more, and they can still find his books in theological libraries. This little book is for the ordinary reader, whether churchgoer or not, and tries to present Michael's ideas, where relevant, in a simple and intelligible way. My own view, for what it is worth, is that Michael will be judged by posterity as one of the greatest Biblical scholars of his generation. He has also been one of the most prolific.

But perhaps I should end with a caveat. Although I have read all but the last of Michael's books, which I list below, this is my book and not his. Were he able to read it, I am sure that he would have suggested amendments, which I would almost certainly have been glad to accept. But some of the views expressed will be mine and only I can be held responsible for them. This chapter is simply the acknowledgement of an immense debt and a long friendship.

Michael's Books and Articles

Michael's eleven published books, now all out of print, are:

Type and History in Acts (SPCK 1964). Written more than forty years ago, Michael would almost certainly want to rewrite parts of this first book in the light of his further research. It attempted to show which stories in the Acts of the Apostles had a historical basis and which could be regarded as midrash.

Midrash and Lection in Matthew (SPCK 1974). Michael's first major book is based on the Speaker's Lectures which he gave at Trinity College, Oxford, between 1969 and 1971. Its reception, or more accurately its non-reception, since its publication passed with very little comment, was a great disappointment. It is, effectively, a commentary on Matthew's Gospel, portraying its author as a Christian Scribe who provides Christian Scripture for a Christian Jewish synagogue. It explains the Jewish tradition of midrashing and introduces the Jewish calendar, for which Matthew's Gospel provides lections.

The Evangelists' Calendar (SPCK 1978). Based on the Speaker's Lectures, as above, but for 1972 and 1973, Michael's second major book is a full statement of his Lectionary Theory. It explains how the Jewish Cycle of weekly and festal readings evolved (the use to which the Old Testament was put in synagogue worship) and how the Synoptic Evangelists wrote their Gospels in response to it. The book received just two or three brief reviews and passed unnoticed into history.

Luke, A New Paradigm (Sheffield Academic Press 1989). Printed in two volumes and running to over 800 pages, this is Michael's longest book by far. It is a brilliant commentary on Luke's Gospel, showing how Luke has first followed Mark, his primary source, and then, in the long Lukan Journey, works over his Matthaean material. It is a wonderful book.

A Tale of Two Missions (SCM Press 1994). Published in paperback, this is the only book which Michael wrote for a general readership. He promised a longer version for his sceptical professional colleagues, but this has been overtaken by illness. The book explains how the church was divided from the beginning between the Jewish (Petrine) congregations and the non-Jewish (Pauline) ones. The books of the New Testament are broadly divided into these two camps. However, the Jewish congregations dwindled and by the fourth century were regarded as heretical. The Paulines became the universal church, from which all present day denominations derive.

In addition Michael has written four books about the Psalter: *The Psalms of the Sons of Korah*, *The Prayers of David*, *The Psalms of Asaph and the Pentateuch*, and *The Psalms of the Return*. He has also written *The Song of Fourteen Songs*, a commentary on the *Song of Songs*. These were all published in the 1980s by the *Journal for the Study of the Old Testament*, an imprint of the Sheffield Academic Press. They are recommended reading in the Cambridge University Theology Faculty and show the liturgical background to the Psalms in the days of the Pilgrim Festivals. Michael's last book was *Isaiah as Liturgy* (Ashgate 2004). He was President of the Society for Old Testament Study in 2001.

Many of Michael's twenty-nine articles anticipate the publication of subsequent books, but one or two are still worth reading. "Characteristics of the Parables in the Several Gospels" (*Journal of Theological Studies* 19, written in 1964) is one of these, and "An Old Friend Incognito" (*Scottish Journal of Theology* 45, written in 1992), which I refer to in the chapter on the Gospel according to John, is another.

[1] *Goulder and the Gospels* by Mark Goodacre (Sheffield Academic Press 1996). Mark has also written *The Synoptic Problem: A Way through the Maze* (T & T Clark International 2001), *The Case against Q* (Trinity Press International, Harrisburg, P.A. 2002), and has jointly edited *Questioning Q* (SPCK 2004) with Nick Perrin. He is currently Associate Professor of New Testament Studies in the Department of Religion at Duke University, North Carolina, and can easily be found on the web.

A BRIEF THEOLOGICAL AUTOBIOGRAPHY

Most of you will have no idea who I am, but may be interested to know where I "come from", theologically, so that you can place this Handbook in context.

Born in 1934 I was a child of the war years and joined the choir of St Mary's, the old Norman church in Guildford, when I was eight. Two evenings a week and twice on Sundays, for Morning and Evening Prayer, with brief termly interruptions while at boarding school, I would be there. St Mary's was Low Church, not of catholic tradition like St Nicholas', at the bottom of Guildford High Street, nor evangelical like St Saviour's, nor Parish Communion, as Holy Trinity was to become. There was no Sunday school and there were no formative influences, except the encouragement of Mr Crickmer, the organist and choirmaster, and the odd smile from a succession of elderly vicars.

I went to Guildford Grammar School at the age of nine, and to Charterhouse when I was thirteen. Boarding at Charterhouse (1947-1951) was a bleak experience, relieved by the consolations of school chapel and the friendship of contemporaries. Don Cupitt, although not in my house and not a close friend at school, was one of these.

The end of the war brought the return to England of a younger generation and, to Guildford, of Walter Boulton, who had been Vicar of the Cathedral in Calcutta. He became Provost of the pro-cathedral, Holy Trinity, and had a strongly held belief that England was at risk of becoming communist. There was a lot of excitement, with Discussion Groups and public debates with high-profile Communist Party members. And it was here, in Guildford, that I had my first experience of the darker side of church life. When the new cathedral was completed Walter Boulton, as Provost, might have expected to have been appointed automatically as the first Dean. But, although popular at Holy Trinity, someone in authority blocked his appointment. There were protests, but to no avail. I learnt, for the first time, how much politicking, and how little openness and accountability, there is in church life. For all the changes that have taken place in the twentieth century, the Church of England remains essentially undemocratic.

Meanwhile I had left school and been articled to a firm of Chartered Accountants in the City. In many ways this has stood me in good stead, since financial competence is often useful, but I never really fitted in and, after four years and much heart-searching, I decided upon ordination. By coincidence I now live in retirement in the Barbican, only a few hundred yards from where this brief City career began. I was not wanted for National Service, on medical grounds, and was then very fortunate to be offered a last-minute place to read theology at St Peter's Hall (now St Peter's College), Oxford. And I was lucky, again, at this point to bring very little theological baggage with me. By contrast with those who arrived in Oxford with loyalties to the Christian Union, or with Anglo-Catholic sympathies, I had little to unlearn.

In retrospect the Oxford Theology School in the 1950s had few original thinkers and I attended very few lectures in the theology faculty. But I was free to attend lectures in other faculties, to study on my own, and to enjoy fringe activities. Austin Farrer, then chaplain of Trinity College, was one of the very few New Testament scholars with really original views. But his brilliant and eccentric lectures, on Saturday mornings, did not bear directly upon the curriculum and were attended by just one or two of us. Dr Croxall, who held no official teaching post in the University, had also just returned from Copenhagen, and led a small seminar on Soren Kierkegaard, for which I shall always be grateful. St Mary's, the University Church, was a lively place on Sunday evenings. Roy Lee was Vicar and a succession of distinguished preachers, including the heroes of the German resistance to Hitler, made a big impression. An English edition of Bonhoeffer's *Letters and Papers from Prison* had also just been published, with their intriguing paragraphs about religionless Christianity. And I belonged to the Student Christian Movement, which is now sadly no more.

Two years' ordination training for graduates was the norm at the time, but I asked to be allowed to spend only a year at Lincoln Theological College and to spend my second year in training at William Temple College, Rugby. Mollie Batten was its inspirational Principal and there was a succession of mid-week and week-end courses for people from all walks of life, but particularly industry, which we were always invited to join. These were the days of Industrial Mission and I had already worked myself, during university vacations, in factories at Scunthorpe and Wolverhampton. Now, at Rugby, I spent a term each studying communism, the psychology of groups, and Christian existentialism. We preached in village churches on Sunday evenings, and did a round of the social work agencies in London.

Alan Webster had become Principal of Lincoln, when I returned for a final term, and he kindly suggested I go to St John's Wood Church, where Noel Perry-Gore was Vicar. As curates we were allowed all the freedom we could have wished and I had a wonderful three years there, organising and leading discussion groups, introducing Christian Aid Week, and meeting interesting, and occasionally distinguished, people. Preaching was a challenge that we relished. It was at St John's Wood Church, too, that Eleanor and I met and became engaged.

My Area Bishop at this juncture wanted me to do a second curacy in Hampstead, but I was ready for a parish of my own and accepted the living of St Luke's, Kingstanding, in Birmingham Diocese, which the Bishop was only too happy for me to fill. At the time it was said to be the largest council housing estate in the country and had been vacant for more than a year. I had twelve very happy years there and made many lifelong friends.

And from Kingstanding, in 1975, I went to St Margaret's, Lee, in Southwark Diocese, a Crown living, and stayed there for twenty-five years until my retirement in 2000. Eleanor was a GP in a well-regarded local practice and ultimately became the Senior Partner. We had no reason to move and most people seemed only too pleased for me to stay. It also enabled us to sustain an immense programme of repair and renovation, which might not otherwise have been possible, and for which much of the credit belongs to a very good friend, Sir Ian Mills. Although an ancient parish (Edmond Halley, the second Astronomer Royal, is buried in the old churchyard), the present church is late Victorian in style and Ian has just completed a book on Victorian church decoration and craftsmanship.

The parish is in South East London and straddles the social divide between Lewisham High Street and Blackheath Village. In churchmanship terms St Margaret's is middle-of-the-road, although church members came from many different backgrounds. We had a Parish Communion on all but the second Sunday of the month, when we sang Morning Prayer. A traditional Evening Prayer followed, with a setting and anthem once a month. Jenny Standage was the Director of Music and we had a very good choir.

I was also at St Margaret's long enough to introduce and sustain several innovations, which have not all survived my departure. One of these was to invite *everyone* to receive communion, whether or not they were confirmed. Only children were excluded, and then only if not formally admitted to communion. Confirmation fits oddly into church life today and can only be regarded as a test of orthodoxy, which thoughtful people of integrity may not wish to take. Ours was a congregation which wished to be inclusive and to allow everyone the freedom to hold their own beliefs. Those who were uncertain might prefer not to come forward, but it seemed odd to invite people to church and then debar them from participation.

Another innovation was to discard the Lectionary and read the individual books of the Bible and Apocrypha in sequence. Over a period of years *every* book was read, several more than once (the Gospels and Pauline Epistles many times), not absolutely in their entirety, but always at some length. We had much longer lessons than are customary elsewhere, or than the Lectionary provides. We used a lectern Bible and it had no dark lines down the edge. It was universally worn! I am a "Bible-based" Christian, as I tell my evangelical friends! More than forty people read lessons and care was taken to help new readers.

One of the people who has influenced me most over the years has been Michael Goulder, and the preceding chapter has explained his contribution to Biblical scholarship and my own debt to him. I have also always admired Don Cupitt, who is a

191

more distant but equally cordial friend (our paths have not crossed to the same extent). He is a hugely knowledgeable philosopher and has written a succession of shortish books, as many as one a year. But his most famous book, *The Sea of Faith*, has given its name to a movement which he founded, and with which I am happy to be identified as a member, the Sea of Faith Network. Its aim is to promote the discussion and understanding of Christian faith amongst those who reject supernaturalism and look to understand religion as a purely human response to life.

Now, in retirement, I have the opportunity to order my thoughts and to present them to a wider readership. My family and friends have been hugely encouraging and two, in particular, with experience of publishing, have helped me enormously in the long and frustrating task of formatting the book. I am grateful to them and to all the others whose eager enquiries have spurred me on.

A FEW DATES

12th cent BC	A possible date for the Exodus from Egypt
10th cent BC	The beginning of the monarchy - Saul, David, and Solomon are successively king. This was the period of Israel's greatest power and influence.
c.930 BC	On Solomon's death the kingdom divides. Jeroboam, the son of Nebat, becomes King of Israel, the Northern Kingdom, with its capital in Samaria, while Rehoboam, David's son, rules the much smaller kingdom of Judah, with its capital in Jerusalem.
722 BC	Samaria falls to the Assyrians, never to be re-established. Only the much smaller kingdom of Judah survives.
9th Ab 586 BC	The destruction of Jerusalem by Nebuchadrezzar and the consequent deportation of its population to Babylon brings the Southern Kingdom of Judah to an end. In its aftermath the Deuteronomic History is completed (1 Samuel - 2 Kings) and the period of the Exile begins. It is the end of an era.
5th cent BC	The return from Exile and the re-building of the Temple in Jerusalem. This marks the beginning of a small, theocratic state, over which Scribes like Ezra and Nehemiah presided. It is the period of influence of the Priestly School, the final editors of the Old Testament.
168-167 BC	The Maccabaean uprising, in response to the profanation of the Temple, leads to a period of relative independence and freedom from Syrian rule. It was during this period that the books of the Apocrypha were written.
AD 26-36	Pontius Pilatus is Procurator of Judaea

AD 30	Most likely date for the Crucifixion of Jesus, but others are possible
AD c.34	Paul's conversion
AD 50-60	Most of Paul's Letters were written during this decade
AD 60-70	Mark's Gospel written during this decade. The persecution of the church begins.
AD 70	The Fall of Jerusalem and massacre of Christians. The church is scattered.
AD 70-80	Matthew's Gospel written during this decade
AD 85	The Blessing of the Sectaries - Christians are excluded from Jewish synagogues
AD 90	Luke's Gospel written around this date
AD 100	John's Gospel probably written in the early second century
AD 100-200	The New Testament Canon gradually takes shape, but is not finalized until the fourth century, or later.
AD 303	The Diocletian persecution of the church begins.
AD 313	Constantine, who has become sole Emperor of both the Eastern and Western Roman Empires, issues the Edict of Milan, which brings the persecution of the church to a final end.
AD 325	Constantine presides at the First Ecumenical Council, held in his summer palace at Nicaea (present day Iznik). All the bishops of the church are invited, although not all attend. The first Conciliar Creed is agreed and rules are introduced for the governance of the church.

INDEX OF BIBLICAL REFERENCES

GENERAL INDEX